HOW TO FEEL
Beautiful

HOW TO FEEL
Beautiful

LIZI JACKSON-BARRETT

Published in 2019 by Welford Publishing
Copyright © Lizi Jackson-Barrett 2019

ISBN: 978-1-9162671-1-4

Illustrations by Gabrielle Vickery Illustration
www.gabriellevickeryillustration.com

Cover photo by Gander Photography
www.ganderphotography.co.uk

Cover photo styled by Stylish Mummy
www.stylishmummy.com

Editing and Design by Fuzzy Flamingo
www.fuzzyflamingo.co.uk

A catalogue for this book is available from the British Library.

For Luke.
Feeling beautiful is easy when I'm with you.

"Feeling beautiful has nothing to do with how you look and everything to do with how you look at yourself."

Lizi Jackson-Barrett

Contents

1. The Importance of Feeling Beautiful   1

2. You Can Stop Now   7

3. What Do You Really, Truly Want?   20

4. Tell It to Your Heart   33

5. You're All Things to All People   46

6. New Habits, New You   61

7. Let's Get Motivated   76

8. Supporters and Saboteurs   89

9. What Is "Beautiful" Anyway?   104

10. Beautiful in the End   114

11. Mind Your Language   120

12. The Right Fairytale   131

Acknowledgements   137

Contact Me   139

About Lizi   141

CHAPTER 1

The Importance of Feeling Beautiful

I was eleven years old the first time I was definitively told I was not beautiful. I was sitting in a science lesson when the teacher walked to the front of the class and asked who wanted to feed the worms we'd been keeping and observing. My hand shot up: this was the kind of special responsibility that meant a lot to me at eleven. Without pausing, he smirked at me. "No Lizi, you might scare them. We'd better have someone pretty do it… come on Katie, up you come." The class roared with laughter and I joined in, trying to retain some dignity. Inside, though, the humiliation was physically painful: a sharp stab of shame that I felt in the pit of my stomach as Katie sauntered to the front of the class to perform the task for which I'd been deemed too unattractive.

The message that I wasn't beautiful stayed with me for the next thirty years. I devoted those decades to trying to make myself invisible. I hid behind "character" clothing; heavy metal t-shirts and black boots with skull chains on them. As I grew up, I changed that for a bland and unnoticeable uniform of muted colours. I dieted

1

(and failed, and dieted and failed, ad nauseum) in the hope I could stop anyone seeing how very *un-beautiful* my fatter-than-average body was. I studied the hair, make-up and affectations of girls like Katie – the girls who *were* beautiful and for whom, it seemed, life was easy. But of course, I wasn't Katie, I was Lizi. My "un-beautifulness" (not quite "ugliness"… it was more subtle than that) made me unworthy of feeding worms: so how could I imagine I was worthy of any of the other hopes and dreams I'd buried at the back of my consciousness?

I bounced from one inappropriate boyfriend to another, willing them to tell me I was beautiful yet knowing they wouldn't because I wasn't. And knowing that I wasn't worthy – that I didn't matter – meant I subconsciously chose boys (and later men) who would reinforce this. It wasn't only my relationships with men that were affected. *Knowing* that I wasn't beautiful meant I felt intimidated by other women. I constantly compared myself to them, and found myself lacking every time.

Positive body image goes far, far deeper than liking your reflection and accepting your bumps, wobbles and flaws. When you believe you're not beautiful, you believe you don't matter. As a confidence coach I see women whose negative body image affects every aspect of their life: their marriage, their friendships, their work, their self-worth. So many of these women come to me with a sense of missed opportunities: how different their lives would be if they were thinner or prettier, or if they had the right hair or nose or legs. Other women are in a state of limbo: wishing they still had the bodies of their youths (when they remember being happier); and waiting for the body they dream they'll have one day (when they imagine they'll be happier again), they feel stuck in a place where, by virtue of not believing they are beautiful the way they are, they can't live a happy life right now.

There's a reason you were drawn to a book called *How to Feel Beautiful*. Because you *know* in your heart, that *feeling* beautiful is very different from *looking* beautiful. That's why you are reading a book written by me rather than one written by a fashion guru, a make-up artist, or a weight loss expert. You *know* that feeling beautiful is something you will achieve not by changing how you look, but by changing how you look at yourself.

Before you begin, let me take a minute to explain how you will get the most from *How to Feel Beautiful*. Ultimately, this is a book about powerful transformations.

You'll read about my own transformation, from feeling ashamed of my appearance for thirty years to loving myself fully, inside and out. But it's also a book about your own transformation. I'll be teaching you how to feel beautiful in much the same way that I learned to, and in the way that I teach my gorgeous clients. You're going to read the stories of my own experiences and those of my clients*, but you also have some work of your own to do.

As you move through the book, you will find challenges and tasks which I have called *Guided*

Reflections. I actually pondered long and hard over what to name these sections: I toyed with "homework" and "written exercises", but they didn't feel very inspiring; and I considered "action steps", but that felt too *busy* for me. I want to create little pockets of time and space for you to stop and look deeply within; to reach understandings about yourself that might have eluded you until now. These aren't a set of exercises for you to tick off on your to-do list before discarding them and moving on to the next job of the day. They are questions designed to make you pause. I'll be asking you to reflect on your experiences, your relationships, your desires and dreams. But I won't be leaving you floundering here: I'll be guiding you through every step. When I work with women as their coach I lovingly and safely challenge them to question the beliefs they hold about themselves and I'll be doing this to you too. So, when you reach a *Guided Reflection* please stop and give yourself the time and space you deserve to explore your thoughts and feelings.

I would like to encourage you to write down your response to each *Guided Reflection*. This will have a much more profound effect on you than simply thinking about them. Committing them to paper makes them tangible and powerful; so please treat yourself to a beautiful notebook in which to chart the journey you're about to start. I also ask you to stick with the questions you find difficult. Don't skip past them or promise you'll come back to them later. The more you want to avoid one of my questions the more likely it is that your answer will hold an essential key in helping you to move forward. Don't be afraid of the difficult work or the challenging feelings that come with it. I can't think of many clients who haven't cried at some point during my work with them; but we can work together to embrace those difficult feelings and understand what they really mean for you.

When you enter into this journey with me fully, with your heart and mind open, by the time you reach the final page you will be a slightly different woman from

"now, for once, it's time to do something **for you.**"

the one you are now. Being a woman in the twenty-first century can often mean trying to be all things to all people; but now, for once, it's time to do something *for you*. So, pour yourself a coffee (or a large merlot if you prefer – I'm not judging!), turn your phone to silent and get comfy. It's time to turn the page and start the next chapter of my book, and the next chapter of your life. It's time to learn how to feel beautiful.

★ All client names have been changed to protect their anonymity. I am so grateful to all the women who entrust me with their happiness and who put their faith in me. You have all inspired me more than you can know.

CHAPTER 2

You Can Stop Now

"What the fuck do I do?"

I sat on the edge of my bed and bent down to pick up the hairbrush that I'd dropped in shock, putting it beside me on the duvet. Lifting my right hand again I paused, centimetres away from my head. I knew I needed to touch it again, but I was scared. *I was just so scared.* I closed my eyes and took a deep breath; and, as I exhaled, my breath was jagged and desperate. My fingertips brushed the strands of frizzy hair aside and found it again… a hairless patch on the side of my head. The sensation of cold fingers on my scalp was nauseating. But I made myself explore it, my eyes filling with tears. The patch was about the size of an egg and dotted with tiny prickles – the remnants of what had been.

My throat was tight as the tears began to fall. I had no idea what to do next. *"What the fuck do I do?"* Around me were piles of clothes, tried on and discarded, as I'd been getting changed to go out for dinner with my girlfriends to celebrate my fortieth birthday. *"Carry on getting ready,"* I told myself. I had to leave soon. I'd been planning to curl my hair and wear it down – something I didn't make the time or effort to do very often – but now that was out of the question. Instead I pulled it back into my usual frizzy ponytail, carefully trying to brush a layer of hair over the patch that made my stomach churn. I checked my reflection… I could still see the gleam of pale skin showing through the gaps in my dark hair. The panic was creeping up and enshrouding me: in my chest I could feel a tight, fast pounding. *I was meant to be going out in an hour, what the fuck was I going to do?*

I had no choice: I didn't want to share my dreadful discovery, but I needed help. Heading downstairs to find my husband Luke, I felt sick. He could see immediately that something was wrong. *"Look!"* I wept, and showed him my head, allowing the tears to flow. Luke wrapped his arms around me and stood calmly and quietly as I cried into his chest. Once I'd managed to regain some control of my sobbing, Luke helped me arrange my ponytail so that my secret (already, so quickly, a source of deep shame) was hidden.

I'd always had a love-hate relationship with my hair. Growing up I despised my thick curls. The coolest girls in school – the girls who I wanted to be – were always the ones with hair that swished. One morning I sat in the school hall listening to the headteacher's assembly, and I noticed two older girls in the row in front of me. One was blonde and the other had light brown hair, and they whispered as they removed their hairbands to re-do their ponytails. The way their long shiny hair fell and swayed as they pulled it back up again had me mesmerised. It was the kind of hair that princesses had. I looked on so enviously at those girls, imagining the friendships, status and popularity that came with having hair like that.

Though I'd already learned quickly, upon starting secondary school, that girls with my hair – *girls who looked like me* – were never going to be given the respect or the opportunities that girls with swishy hair got. My experience in the science lesson, desperate to feed the class's worms but being cut down by my thoughtless teacher telling me that my face would frighten them, told me everything I needed to know about the way others perceived me. Thirty years later I can still clearly hear his voice. *"No Lizi, you might scare them. We'd better have someone pretty do it… come on Katie, up you come."* I still wonder what was going through Katie's mind in that instant as she sauntered to the front of the class, her mousey ponytail swishing behind her.

That was the moment that I knew the girls who looked like Katie – girls who were beautiful – were *better than me*. I didn't look like them. I had short, thick, dark curls (one boy nicknamed me "pubes"); I wore huge glasses; my front teeth were too big and stuck out. I didn't wear the right trainers or roll my school skirt up to make it short enough. I didn't look like the Katies of this world, and I believed with all my heart that I needed to. And so began thirty years of trying to change the way I looked. I started and restarted countless diets – knowing that the body I had was too fat to ever be considered good enough. For three decades I tried to change my shape; my skin; my face; my hair. I waxed and plucked; I straightened and curled; I sprayed and smoothed. None of this came naturally to me, but I knew that my most important goal in life was to look as much like "the Katies" as I could. I'd never look *just* like them of course. I knew that. I'd never be as pretty, as slim, as cute, as desirable, as beautiful, *as swishy*... but I knew I had to try. And I knew that I could never give up on this mission, no matter how futile it felt.

"I waxed and plucked; I straightened and curled; I sprayed and smoothed."

In my late teens, after years of cutting my curls short, I grew them out – and the longer my hair got the more I liked it. It would never swish of course – that wasn't for girls like me – but I learned how to make it look good. It was a time-consuming task and not one I prioritised often, but when I did, I would wear my meticulously-styled ringlets with pride. In my twenties and thirties I experimented with colour. Blonde highlights; coppery reds; shocking pink: turning my hair into a fun accessory gave me a whole new way of enjoying it. When I met Luke at thirty-six, I had purple streaks, which he loved.

But here we were, just four years later, standing in the living room as I cried into his chest, while he continued to reassure me that the bald patch wasn't visible and that my friends would be none the wiser that evening.

Within six weeks almost all the hair on my head was gone. It had fallen out in a strange pattern, firstly forming a bald circle around my crown with one long ridiculous tuft of hair still sprouting from its centre. Soon after that my hairline had receded, and the hair above each ear had thinned drastically. And the pain was like nothing I had ever experienced. It felt as it might do if someone were to drag you around by your ponytail for hours on end: sometimes so excruciating that it brought me to tears. I had been to a doctor: the alarmingly quick progress of the alopecia led my parents to pay for me to see a private dermatologist who prescribed steroids. Steroid shampoo; steroid cream; steroid tablets… I used it all, but nothing would halt the shedding.

Every day I charted the losses with pictures taken of the top of my head, which I sent to a few close friends in a grim and macabre photo diary. I never showed my face in those photos though – I know now that I was trying to disassociate myself from the horror happening on my head. I wanted those friends to see the trauma I was living through, but I didn't want them to see it *as part of me.*

Brushing my remaining hair into a high ponytail each day – pulling the strands up from the back and sides to cover the worst of the baldness – was a miserable affair. At times it seemed like the brush held more of my hair than my head did, and I took a kind of gloomy pleasure in continuing to brush until there was nothing left to come out that day. It was early December so at least the season allowed me to wear a woolly hat every time I left the house. I'll always be grateful that my hair fell out in winter.

During those early weeks of alopecia, it felt as though I would never stop crying. My sorrow was all-consuming. I felt the same deep sense of grief as I did when my grandparents died. I had a moment when I woke each morning and my world felt normal, but within seconds I would remember the reality; and then the earth shifted to an unnatural angle and everything was wrong. I tried to remain upbeat for my eight-year-old twins but when they weren't looking the tears flowed freely. I cried in my car. *A lot.* Once the children were at school I drove away, locked the doors, and howled. I would lay my head on my steering wheel and wail, a deep, rasping sob from the depths of my belly.

Everything was changing. *I* was changing. I was changing in a way that I didn't want to, at an alarming speed, and there was nothing I could do about it. I was sad and angry and miserable and despairing… but most of all I was scared.

I was scared that Luke wouldn't fancy me any more. The first time Luke and I saw each other in person after meeting on a dating app, I knew within seconds that I didn't stand a chance with him. He was so handsome – so utterly gorgeous – that I felt certain that I could only possibly be a disappointment to him. I was amazed that his kiss at the end of the night said otherwise. Three years later we got married. Luke didn't only become my husband, he became my children's father. My previous marriage had been an abusive one for both me and them, and we had gone through some difficult years together before Luke came into our lives. Finally, we were getting the "happy ever after" that we deserved.

But now, just six months after our wedding, this beautiful man was facing life with a bald wife. I pictured myself wearing a wig to bed and imagined the humiliation of it slipping off during sex. When I sobbed out this vision to Luke on the phone (from my car – my favourite place to cry) he asked me in bemusement why I would wear a wig in bed. I see now that this was because for Luke I hadn't changed. I was the same woman he fell in love with and the same woman he married, and for him a lack of hair made very little difference. But, of course, I couldn't see that then. All I could see was that my darling, gorgeous, sexy husband – my handsome prince, who deserved a swishy-haired princess – was stuck with an embarrassment of a wife whom he'd never truly desire again.

I was more than scared – I was terrified. I was terrified that I would never feel pretty again. I had devoted three decades to trying to change my physical appearance. For thirty years I had ploughed so much of my energy and emotion into trying to look different – attempting to look like the beautiful women of this world. Trying to look like the Katies, with their effortless swishy hair. And now I had to admit defeat. It had all been for nothing. Because after thirty years of trying, I was further from looking like them than I'd ever been before. I was terrified that I would have to give up on the idea of transforming my appearance: give up on the dream that one day, if I just tried hard enough, I might be able to be beautiful too. Because giving up on that dream meant accepting I was always going to look like this.

Until one night in mid-December – after Luke had lovingly shaved off the last remaining hairs on my head – I lay in bed in the dark. Luke was sleeping deeply next to me and I stared at the ceiling, the tears running down my cheeks and pooling around my ears, soaking my pillow. I was crying for all those wasted years. I was crying for the energy I had poured into trying to look beautiful, and I was crying that it had all been for nothing. And then a thought formed.

"You can stop now."

I had never before imagined that I could… just… stop. It was a strangely thrilling thought. I had no idea what I would find to occupy that energy if I didn't spend it on trying to change; and I had no idea if it was possible to learn to love myself exactly as I was – but in that moment I knew that it was what I wanted to do. Thirty years of believing I couldn't be beautiful – of believing I wasn't good enough; that I needed to change; that I was too ugly to feed the worms – had been exhausting. And now I was giving myself permission to stop.

The truth is, I had no choice. My sudden alopecia and the way it changed my appearance so quickly meant I *had* to stop on my endless mission to look like the swishy-haired girls. I *had* to stop trying to be something I wasn't, and I *had* to learn to see myself with new eyes. I had no choice, but you do. You can *choose* to stop trying to look fundamentally different from how you already are. You can choose to stop believing that you're not good enough. You can choose to stop telling yourself that your life will be better if you change how you look.

You can stop now.

I'm going to say that again. Because it's going to take a while for it to sink in for you.

You can stop now.

For years – decades, even – you've bought into the narrative that as a woman the most important thing you can do is look pretty. You have resigned yourself to the idea that your body exists to please others, and that the most important responsibility in your life is to be visually appealing. You've invested innumerable hours, immeasurable energy and inestimable money in trying to look different so that other people can relax when they look at you. You have exhausted yourself trying to look the way you think you're *supposed* to look. *But you can stop now.*

You compare yourself to other women. You compare yourself to the women who seem to have it all together; the women whose husbands appear to dote on them; the women whose children are always in clean and ironed clothes; the women who are taller and thinner than you; the women who walk effortlessly in heels; the women with manicured nails and fluttery eyelashes and swishy hair. You compare yourself to every kind of woman and you find yourself lacking. *But you can stop now.*

You presume that the same comparison works both ways. You envisage other women judging you negatively, based on how you look. You assume that those women think you're not as good as them; that you should tidy your hair and freshen up your wardrobe and find time for make up every morning. You imagine that other women take one look at you and believe you are not the kind of woman they want to be friends with. *But you can stop now.*

It has become ingrained in you to reject compliments. It's a pattern that's become so entrenched that you barely even recognise them as compliments; instead, you've formed a solid armour against them so positive comments bounce off you like arrows. Compliments embarrass you because you can't believe them yourself, and it's hard to imagine they were given sincerely – so you brush them aside or turn them into a joke. *But you can stop now.*

You have fallen into the habit of apologising for physically existing. You squeeze past strangers' chairs in restaurants, saying sorry for making them edge forwards a little more. You try to make yourself smaller on the train so that your body doesn't encroach onto someone else's seat. And you have developed the habit of making self-deprecating jokes, because you're sure it's what other people must be thinking about you and it's easier to pretend you think it's funny than acknowledge how deeply it wounds you. You laugh that you have no self-control around food because you're scared that's what others believe to be true. *But you can stop now.*

The vocabulary you've developed to describe yourself is almost exclusively negative, especially when it comes to the way you look. You casually refer to your wobbly thighs, your greasy hair, your chipped nails and wonky teeth; and the voice in your head is even less complimentary. It uses words like "stupid", "fat", "undesirable", "ugly"... and you believe it. You would never dream of using such unkind words to refer to another woman, yet you only know how to describe yourself negatively. The thought of calling yourself beautiful seems almost laughable. *But you can stop now.*

You have spent your life feeling about your body the way you've been told you're *supposed* to feel about your body. You live in a world where women are expected to feel ashamed of every stretch mark; any loose skin; everything that wobbles. You're meant to despise boobs that are too small and boobs that are too big; teeth with gaps and thighs without them. You're in a society that tells you you're supposed to feel deficient and lacking, and that you are meant to resent any part of you that doesn't match up to the arbitrary set of standards called "beauty". You've been programmed to feel negatively towards every imperfect part of your beautiful self; without ever stopping to examine how you *really truly* feel about your body. *But you can stop now.*

You don't need to feel bad that you have spent your life doing all these things. We all do them. It's part of being human and being a woman and living in the society that we live in. It's part of living in the appearance-obsessed, selfie-saturated twenty-first century. You haven't let yourself down by spending all those years trying to look different and believing your appearance is a disappointment to everyone. But you know what? *You can stop now.*

It's time to be done with that. Now you can think about loving yourself the way you are without having to change anything. And all that time and energy and money you were putting into trying to look different can now be used for other things. Things that *truly* make you happy and fulfilled; things that nurture your soul; things that make your heart sing. Things that make it unnecessary to compare yourself to other women because you know you are *enough* in every way. Things that make you proud of your physical, emotional and spiritual being. Things that make you confident in everything that makes you who you are.

It all begins with learning how to feel beautiful.

And now you can start.

CHAPTER 3

What Do You Really, Truly Want?

You know what you want, right? *Are you sure?* What we *say* we want isn't always what we *really, truly* want. Our true wants, hopes, dreams and desires are often buried: because we tell ourselves to stop hankering after the impossible, or because we think we need to be sensible and grown-up, and put our energies into the realities of day-to-day living rather than our deepest yearnings.

So telling me what you want is a start, certainly – and it's what I'm going to ask you to do shortly. It's the starting point for all the clients that I work with. They want to be slimmer; to shop in the fashionable stores; to look in the mirror and be happy with their reflections. They want to have more energy; to learn how to say "no" and to prioritise themselves once in a while. They want to feel more in control of their lives. They want to feel beautiful. Every woman I've ever helped as a coach has come to me wanting at least some of these things, and I know you want them too. So it's a good start: telling me what you want. And it's what I'd like you to do now. It's time to open the notebook you will be using on your journey towards feeling beautiful.

Guided Reflection 1:

At the top of your first page write: *"What do I want?"* And then write whatever comes to mind. You want to feel beautiful, yes, but what does this mean to you? What do you want as a result of feeling beautiful? Nobody else ever needs to see this list, so be completely honest. And set it out in a way that feels right to you – whether you choose bullet points, a spider diagram, full paragraphs of prose, or something else entirely – go with your instincts on this.

- What will feeling beautiful look like for you?
- What will it be like when you have achieved this dream?
- How will you look? How will you feel?
- What will people see when they notice you?
- Can you visualise a moment when it will all come together and you will know, without a doubt, that you have achieved exactly what you wanted?

Imagine I could wave a magic wand and give you what you want: what would it look like? Write it all down. Describe it. *Tell me what you want.*

One of my gorgeous clients, Anne, came to me telling me she knew what she wanted. What she desired more than anything, she said, was to lose weight. She was certain that reducing her size would lead to her feeling beautiful. She was irritated and angry with herself because she kept sabotaging her weight loss by eating food that didn't fit with her diet plan. I could hear the frustration in her voice as she told me, "I don't understand it! I can see my end goal so clearly in my mind – I can visualise it exactly! So it's not as though I don't have the right motivation."

I asked Anne to describe the end point she could see so vividly. She told me how she pictured herself walking into a party, three sizes smaller than she currently was. It was a classy and sophisticated event and she was wearing a long red dress that showed her new slim figure. She told me how everyone at the party would look round at her in amazement as she walked in; gasping in admiration at Anne's transformation. They would be so impressed at the work she had put into becoming this gorgeous, elegant woman. Anne could describe every detail of her visualised goal, so why – she asked – why wasn't she more motivated to stick to her diet and get the body she needed to make her beautiful dream a reality? Why did she set herself up to fail, again and again, each time despairing a little more; *hating* herself a little more?

But there was something missing from Anne's dream scenario, and it turned out to be the key to unlocking an important realisation. I asked her to tell me why *this* – the party, the admiration, the red dress – was the goal she had chosen and she stopped in her tracks. Anne was clear on the "what", but not on the "why". Eventually, after a long period of silence, she said, "I don't know. It's what we're all supposed to want, isn't it?"

And of course, she is right. For me there was a very clear comparison to be drawn, which you might have noticed too. Anne's big dream sounds so much like a scene from the Disney movie *Cinderella*, don't you think? The grand entrance, the beautiful gown, the appreciative gasps. And, if you're anything like me and Anne, you'll have grown up listening to all the old fairy tales and watching Disney movies, being fed the same narrative again and again. *Beauty equals good, ugly equals bad.* Being beautiful means being wanted, desired, loved and valued. And the most important thing we were shown, was for *others* to see our external beauty – it is only then that the "happy ever after" can truly be possible. Cinderella was the same girl at the ball as she was in her rags at home: but she needed the physical transformation for her prince to recognise that beauty. The message is clear. So, of course, Anne was right: that "Cinderella moment" *is* what every girl is supposed to want.

So Anne told me what she wanted, just like you have in your notebook. But what did Anne *really, truly* want? The secret, it emerged, lay not in the details of what her goal *looked* like, but rather what it *felt* like. I encouraged Anne to put the mental image of the party to one side. And I asked her what her success would *feel* like. I'll reveal what she said shortly, but first I'd like you to try doing exactly what Anne did, by answering the same questions I asked her. It's time to open your notebook again and write a new heading: *"What I really, truly want"*.

Guided Reflection 2:

Imagine you have achieved your goal. You have succeeded and you now feel beautifully comfortable and confident in your own skin. All the work you've put into this journey and transformation has paid off, and now you can enjoy the results.

When you wake up in the morning, what is your first clue that things are different from how they are now?
Where are you? How does your body feel? How did you sleep? Is anyone else in the house with you? What can you hear? What's the first thought that enters your mind, and the first thing you do when you get out of bed?

When you get dressed for the day ahead, what are you wearing?
Is it smart or casual, or a different style altogether? How do you feel about your clothes? What has made you pick this outfit? How does it compare to what you wore the previous day and will wear the next day? When you check your reflection what do you see? How do you feel?

Who will you spend your day with?
Are you with colleagues, friends, family or perhaps alone? What is your relationship with the people in your life? How do they make you feel about yourself?

What will your leisure time be like?
And how often will it happen? Will you have time for self-care and for fun? What activities will be part of your life that bring you joy? And what will that joy feel like to you?

How will other people describe you?
When people talk about you to others what kinds of words will they use? What influence will you have on the lives of those around you and how much of your time and energy will be spent on other people? How do you make others feel?

When you go to bed how are you feeling about your day?
What have you achieved? How are you feeling both physically and emotionally?

There may be other questions that come into your mind that you intuitively know play a part in this idyllic picture of your future. Listen to your instincts and write them down.

I promised you that I would reveal what Anne said when I asked her these same questions: and it's safe to say she surprised herself. But as you have probably just discovered, there's a world of difference between telling me what your beautiful future *looks* like and what it *feels* like; and this was certainly the case for Anne. It turned out that her perfect future didn't involve ballgowns and parties after all.

What Anne *actually* wanted was to barely think about the shape and size of her body. Her dream future involves getting out of bed feeling energised and rested, putting on some jeans and a t-shirt, feeling content with her reflection, and getting on with her day. That was what Anne *really, truly* wanted. Which, of course, is the complete opposite of the picture she had been visualising to try to motivate herself. She had been telling herself all along that what she was *supposed* to want was to be judged by her appearance. But what she actually wanted was for her appearance to be of little consequence. Anne told me that the overriding feeling she wanted to achieve was *comfortable* – both emotionally and physically. Not "glamourous", "stunning", "admired"… or even "slim". She wanted to feel comfortable in her own skin, and comfortable in her clothing. Anne had reached the realisation that *looking* beautiful and *feeling* beautiful were often two different things… and she'd been chasing the wrong one.

Anne's story is one I see again and again with the wonderful clients I work with. Almost every time, they come to me believing that to feel beautiful and confident they need to change how they look. Often their initial goals are about making time to go to the gym or have their hair done more often. But then, just like Anne, they discover that what needs to change isn't how they look but how they feel about themselves, inside and out.

And that is certainly a realisation I discovered too. For thirty years I believed I needed to change how I look, and that would then lead to me feeling beautiful. I was convinced that if I could just have a flat tummy; long, thin legs; and shiny, swishy hair, all my troubles would be solved. I'd have higher self-esteem and would feel confident and gorgeous. But I was wrong: I *still* have a big, saggy tummy and short, fat legs (and as for the frizzy hair I hated so much… well, you know how that one ends!). But instead of the self-loathing that used to come with the body parts that are so far from perfect, I now feel beautiful and confident in my own skin. Nothing has changed except the way I see myself.

"feeling beautiful has nothing to do with how you lOOK and everything to do with how you look at yourself."

27

If that wasn't proof enough that you don't need to change how you look to feel gorgeous, let me tell you about another client, Holly. When I first met Holly, I was a little in awe. She was just so damn glamorous! Tall, elegant and curvy; always in stunning designer clothes, flawless make-up and the swishiest hair I'd ever seen. But Holly's self-esteem was desperately low; she exhausted herself trying to make people like her; she was constantly insecure and anxious, and she sobbed beside me as she spoke about how unattractive she felt. Holly is one of many women I've helped who one might imagine *must* feel confident in her own beauty. But I've said it before, and I'll say it again: feeling beautiful has nothing to do with how you look and everything to do with how you look at yourself.

Guided Reflection 3:

It's time now to write down a clear goal. We're going to call it your "True Goal" because it's borne from a much deeper understanding than many of your previous goals.

Look back at Guided Reflection 2 and ask yourself exactly what it is that you want to achieve, and why. Anne, for example, ended up with a True Goal that said:

"I will feel positive at the start of each day, and I will feel comfortable and confident wearing jeans and a t-shirt. I will stop putting myself down and I will feel happy in my own body. I will make time for my own self-care because I know I am worth it."

Now you try it. Write "My True Goal" as your heading and try to put it into words. Write "I will" rather than "I want to" or "I wish"… write it with conviction and a belief that it *will* happen!

After realising her True Goal, Anne acknowledged that the truth of her original vision actually terrified her! She knew that the reality of walking into that party in her elegant red dress would have involved hours of getting ready: she'd have had to invest time and money on her hair and make-up; she'd be uncomfortable in a pair of control knickers and painful shoes… and all those eyes on her as she made her entrance actually made her feel anxious, panicky, and under way too much pressure. How the dream *looked*, it turned out, was very different from how the dream *felt*. Of course, Anne had really known this all along deep down, though it took some work with me to bring this into her conscious mind, and this was why she'd been sabotaging her plans to achieve her goal. Deep down she actively wanted to *avoid* the scenario she'd been telling herself to work towards; so far from it being motivating as she'd intended, it was actually pushing her further and further from her weight loss goals.

And so it turned out that Anne still *did* want to lose weight – but for personal comfort and quiet confidence, rather than for public admiration and a flamboyant display of beauty. Once she fully understood this and revised what her visualisation of "success" looked like she found the motivation that had been eluding her all along. Anne had spent years trying and failing to achieve her "Cinderella moment", simply because she had spent her life believing that was what she was supposed to want. But in that one important conversation I had with her, she gave herself permission to *stop* expending all her energy on *the wrong thing* and start focusing on achieving the feelings that would really make her happy.

The parallels with my own story are clear. As I've described in Chapter 1, I came to the same understanding as Anne did: I was using my energy on the wrong things – and it was an understanding that changed my life. So, let me ask you this: are you doing what Anne and I did?

Go back to your notebook and compare what you've written about *what you want* (in Guided Reflection 1) to what you've written about *what you really, truly want* (in Guided Reflection 2). How much energy do you put into the first list? Remember, of course, that "energy" can take many forms. It might be physical energy you are wasting: running from place to place in the pursuit of the goals on your list. Or maybe it is emotional energy: crying for the dreams you've lost or are yet to experience;

feeling frustrated with your lack of success or envious of others. You've probably also invested your financial energy into that "want to" list: paying for diet plans, makeovers, courses, gifts and gadgets. And, of course, your thoughts are also energy. Have you been directing them to the right place? What would it be like to lovingly and firmly close the door on your first list and transfer your energies to the second?

Remember, the aim of this book is to help you *feel* beautiful, and the first stage to getting there is to let go of all the pictures of success that have been handed down to you. I believed for thirty years that I'd find my beauty in a flat tummy, thin legs and swishy hair. Anne had believed that her beauty was to be found in her Cinderella moment. We were both wrong. And once we learned that our beauty could be felt in a completely different way, we were both able to start working towards that powerful, transformative feeling.

You don't need to feel regretful about the energy you have poured into your first list: the goals you *thought* you wanted. I don't want you to feel bad if you have just discovered that you were working towards a goal that won't make you feel beautiful after all. Instead, embrace this new understanding you have. See it as a positive, that you can now redirect yourself onto the path that will lead to you where you *really, truly* want to be.

Women are influenced by other women: we always have been. Whether it is Cinderella or other mums in the playground: we see what we think other women have and we imagine how they must feel about themselves; and we allow that to tell us what *we* are supposed to want and how *we* are supposed to feel about ourselves. But now it's time for you to gently put those beliefs about yourself aside. Forget about what you thought you wanted; let's take the next step together so you can finally achieve the True Goal that you really, truly want.

CHAPTER 4

Tell It to Your Heart

In Chapter 3 you did some very important work: you rejected the narrative you've lived with about the goals you're *supposed* to want and began to visualise the life you really want to be living. This book is about learning how to feel beautiful, but as you're starting to see this means something different to everyone. For some women it's about the Cinderella moment: walking into the grand ball with all eyes on you. For some women it's comfortable jeans and barely even thinking about how you look. And for you it means something different still.

But I'm guessing that there's a huge gap between where you are now and where you want to be. In the last chapter you defined a clear and meaningful True Goal which will result in you feeling truly beautiful, but the likelihood is that at the moment it still feels a bit abstract. I know that right now a life where you feel confident in your own beauty might still feel unreachable and difficult to believe in. In this chapter we're going to work on connecting you with your goals on a deeper level. Once you can truly visualise them as part of your future they will become easier to reach and you'll feel inspired and motivated to achieve them.

I fully appreciate that I'm becoming annoying here! I asked you to tell me what you want. So you did. But I didn't accept that, and I asked you to tell me what you *really* want. You trusted me, went with it, and found a new layer of desires. But here I am again, *still* banging on about defining your goals. How irritating! But you know what? I'm not sorry! This chapter is about connecting with the goals you set out in Chapter 3 on a more emotional level. I don't doubt for a minute that you really, truly want the goals you've now got written in your notebook; but wanting them isn't enough. You have to *feel* them.

I know what it's like to have spent ten or twenty years or more longing for a goal that feels constantly out of reach – but this time is going to be different. Before you start turning your dreams into reality you have to do the emotional groundwork, and this is probably what's been missing until now. You've made a brilliant start by beginning to visualise the reality of achieving your goal, but now we need to go deeper and understand *why* you want it.

Chapter 3 was about learning what you really desire and connecting to that goal *with your mind*. This chapter is all about connecting to your goal *with your heart*.

You have started creating a picture of what life will look like when you reach your goal of feeling beautiful, but now we're going to broaden that picture into a full and deep understanding of the true effect it will have on your life. I always knew, for example, that I wanted to feel confident in my own body. I went through the same process I'm guiding you through: I reflected on what feeling like that *really* meant for me and what it would be like to live a life where I wasn't constantly giving myself a hard time for not being enough (*pretty enough, thin enough, cool enough, swishy enough*). What I *hadn't* fully understood is that achieving that goal would have a powerful impact on so much more of my life than I could have imagined.

Take my work as a coach, for example. If I hadn't been through the transformation that I have – experiencing the lowest point of self-loathing and the incredible highs of contentment in my own body – I never could have built my successful coaching business, helping hundreds of women to develop their self-esteem and confidence. Or take my marriage as another example. If I hadn't worked through the sense of desperate inadequacy to reach the point of feeling every bit deserving of my gorgeous husband, we wouldn't have the beautiful and intimate connection we enjoy now. And my relationship with my children has changed for the better too. I hadn't fully appreciated the wonderful effect it can have on children to live with a mum who speaks positively about her own body *and means it*: although I'd known this in theory, it has been gratifying and truly special to see the impact on their confidence in their own beautiful bodies.

So, achieving my goal of feeling confident in my own skin *did* do what I hoped and imagined it would do, because it enabled me:

- to stop feeling miserable about my imperfections;
- to stop being apologetic for my physical being;
- to start experimenting with my own style in terms of clothes, jewellery and make-up;
- and to direct my energies to emotional self-care rather than constant diets.

But achieving my goal also resulted in so much more than I expected, because it also enabled me:

- to feel like a great mum and increase my children's self-esteem;
- to enjoy a relationship with my husband that makes me deeply happy;
- and to build a successful business in which I help other women to feel confident and beautiful too.

If I'd known about that second list at the outset and been able to visualise those outcomes it would have been immensely easier to achieve the goal that would lead to them being a reality. That's why I'm asking you to explore your goals much more deeply now: so that you can understand the true value of getting there.

Guided Reflection 4:

You're going to start thinking more deeply about the potential effects of achieving your True Goal. Get out your notebook and start writing your answers to these questions:

When you achieve your True Goal and feel truly beautiful, what else might change in your life?
- And then what?
- And then what?
- And then what?

Keep the thread going for as long as you can! Are you feeling confused? Let me give you an example of a conversation I had with one of my clients, Alice:

When you achieve your True Goal, what else might change in your life?
Alice: "I'll stop worrying about what other people think of me."
- And then what?
  Alice: "And then I'll push myself out of my comfort zone and do things that I've avoided until now for fear of judgement."
- And then what?
  Alice: "And then I'll start sharing my photography on social media without being scared of negative feedback."

- And then what?
  Alice: *"And then I might have success and find that people love what I do."*
- And then what?
  Alice: *"And then I might be able to start the photography business I dream of."*

Do you see how it works? You need to keep an open mind and dream big with this. Once you've done as many "and then what…" answers as you can think of, start again with a new "when I achieve my True Goal…".

Are you surprised at the potential that opens up to you when you get to your goal? Your initial aim was around feeling beautiful, or at least feeling comfortable in your body, but the opportunities that will open up for you are beyond anything you could have imagined. Alice had no idea that her lack of confidence in the way she looked was stopping her from creating the career she had dreamed of; and she felt understandably sad when she realised how different her life might look if she'd had more body confidence and self-esteem when she was younger. But equally she was excited to see that, by working on the way she saw herself, she was creating opportunities for happiness and success that were beyond anything she'd imagined.

I wish I had recognised those opportunities in

myself, when I was trying and failing for all those years to feel beautiful in my own skin. Sometimes I wish I could go back in time and tell myself that it will all be all right. I wish I could tell myself *how* all right it will be. My goal has always been essentially the same, for as long as I can remember. It was always a variation on wanting to feel beautiful. I always wanted to feel like I could walk into a room with confidence; I wanted to feel desirable; I wanted to receive compliments and admiration; I wanted to feel happy in my body.

I remember feeling like my goals were so intangible that they were barely worth thinking about: I know you might have been feeling this way too. And I know there were so many times I would have benefited from a crystal ball to show me that I didn't need to worry. I wish I could have told my old self that I *would* end up feeling beautiful and that I'd had the power to feel like that all along, if only I'd known how.

When I was fifteen, for example, I asked out a boy in my year at school. I didn't think I was pretty or desirable: in fact, I was certain that in comparison with the swishy-haired sporty girls I wasn't worth looking at. However, Steve and I had shared a kiss at a recent party and so I thought I might stand a chance: at least it was unlikely he found me repulsive. So, I asked him if he'd like to go out with me, and he said he wanted to think about it. The next day Steve came to school and handed me a two-page letter detailing all the ways I would need to physically change before he would consider me as a girlfriend. I remember even now, twenty-six years later, the words: "straighten your hair and get a brace on those teeth of yours". Steve had shown the letter to some of his friends before giving it to me, which meant my humiliation and hurt was compounded by the laughter and teasing I had to endure.

I would love to go back to that Lizi and tell her that Steve's words were ugly, not her. That his behaviour was driven by his own need for acceptance and approval from his peers, and wasn't about Lizi at all. I want to tell 15-year-old me that she dealt with that attack with grace and dignity, but that she did not deserve to be treated so callously. I want to tell her she deserves so much better. I would tell her to see the beauty in her spirit and her tenacity; in her enthusiasm and her joy for life. I want her to know that she *is* beautiful, despite Steve's attempts to persuade her otherwise.

Or I'd go back to thirty-four year old me – only seven years ago, but such a different version of myself from who I am now. I was newly divorced and venturing into the world of online dating, and had been on a few dates with Rick. I hadn't felt much of an emotional or intellectual connection, but he was handsome and had a gorgeous Scottish accent, so I'd decided to stick with it and enjoy having some fun with this sexy and uncomplicated man. One evening, in a restaurant, Rick took both my hands in his and gazed at me across the candlelight before gently murmuring, "You would be so pretty if you lost some weight." I literally did not know how to respond, and in fact a big part of me thought Rick's words were true: I *would* be prettier if I lost weight. I did know it was rude of Rick to have said so, but I didn't see how I could stand up for myself in the face of such a brutal truth. So I kissed him. And dated him for two more months.

I would love to go back to that Lizi and tell her that she is bloody gorgeous. Her new-found freedom after leaving her abusive marriage had given her a sparkle that had previously been dulled by years of emotional torment by her former husband. She was just beginning to rediscover who she was and what made her happy. I want to tell her that she is allowed to walk away from people and situations that make her feel bad. I want to tell her that there *is* a man out there waiting for her who thinks she's beautiful exactly the way she is. I want to show her the beauty in her courage and resilience; and in her loving generosity. I want her to know that she *is* beautiful, and that Rick's rude and hurtful words are meaningless.

And I'd go back to the Lizi of October 2017, on the day she found her first bald patch whilst getting ready for her fortieth birthday party. I want to step in while she sobs into her husband's chest and whisper into her ear that losing her hair is going to be one of the best things to happen to her. I want to show her that going bald will make her understand what it truly means to be and feel beautiful and that it will give her the power to cast off all the old beliefs about herself. I want *that* Lizi to know that her world isn't ending: in fact, it's beginning. In that very moment the most exciting, happy and wonderful stage of her life is starting, although it feels to her like the most horrific thing imaginable. I want to tell her that alopecia will give her the means to connect with women all over the world, inspiring them and empowering them to embrace their own unique beauty. I want to look her in the eye and tell her how much I love being bald, and all that baldness has brought me. I want her to know that she has always been beautiful, but it's going to take losing her hair to see it for herself.

Shortly I am going to ask you to do what's possibly

the hardest Guided Reflection in this book. You're going to mentally transport yourself forwards five years and write a letter to your current self from your future self. Fifteen-year-old me; thirty-four-year-old me; and forty-year-old me would have all loved so much to receive a letter from Future Me. There were so many things I would have liked to have known which would have undone so much of the pain and uncertainty I was feeling.

You're going to imagine that some of the opportunities you've uncovered in Guided Reflection 4 have become a reality, and that Future You wants to come back in time to reassure you. Because it's *you*, you know everything that's in your head right now. You know your dreams and your fears. You know the worries that keep you awake at night. And you know how the next five years pan out, and that everything will end up being wonderful.

You might want to keep a box of tissues handy for this work: there's a good chance you'll shed a few tears. Spend a couple of minutes first sitting quietly with your eyes closed: centre yourself and tune in to your thoughts and feelings. Listen to your heart. And then begin.

Guided Reflection 5:

Imagine you have received a letter from a future version of yourself. It's a You who has achieved your current goals. The potential you began to understand in Guided

Reflection 4 has been realised: it's no longer a list in a notebook, but is your lived reality. What does the letter say?

- What does successful, happy Future You acknowledge about the way you feel about yourself right now?
- What dreams and desires does she know are in your heart?
- What does she want to tell you about the worries that are holding you back?
- How have the goals you've written in your notebook become a reality over the next five years?
- What positive effect has it had on the life that Future You is living?

Take your time with this, and let your imagination go to work. The more detail you put into your description of your future life the more motivated and inspired you will be to make it a reality.

I know that wasn't easy, but it was a really important step: you're now connecting with your goal on a very deep, emotional level. And it's through that heart-felt connection that your goal will become your reality.

Over the last two chapters you have been laying the groundwork to bring about a huge transformation in your life. You started reading this book to learn how to feel beautiful, and you're discovering that the path to achieving that involves making some profound changes to the way you see yourself and your goals. In the next chapters you're going to start thinking about how to make that a reality, but for now take a minute to appreciate all you have achieved since you started this book. Look back over your notebook and see the progress you have made. You are doing brilliantly, my lovely. I'm so proud of what you're accomplishing right now, and you should be too.

CHAPTER 5

You're All Things to All People
(But what's left for you?)

"Tell me about yourself."

What do you say when you're asked this question? Try answering it now, but don't overthink it. Write down in your notebook a list of five things you might say in response. *Don't read on until you've done it.*

I mean it.

Stop reading.

Write your answers.

And then come back and read on.

OK... I'm going to make a guess: most of your replies aren't about you at all, but are about *who you are to others*. Am I right?

Not so long ago I was no different: my self-defined identity has so often been shaped by who I am to others. A mum to twins, and later a single mum and an abused ex-wife. A daughter still so reliant on her parents for so much. A dutiful granddaughter, wanting to do right by my grandparents. A friend: the one who makes the others laugh; who listens and gives advice. A teacher; a

46

big sister; an auntie. And then an adoring wife and loving step-mum. Those roles were – and are – so important to me. They encapsulate so many of my life experiences; my values and core beliefs. The different roles I played in my life had, over the years, grown to define who I was as a woman. And you almost certainly have roles that feel identity-defining to you too: I'm going to ask you to think about them now.

Guided Reflection 6:

In your notebook draw the shape of a woman, to represent you. You don't need to be an artist for this – a stick woman or a rough outline is fine! Leave space to write inside the woman later. Around the outside of her draw circles to represent the different roles that make up who you are and label each one. For example:

Once you've finished, continue reading: you'll come back to this shortly.

Those roles are important to us and we can – and should – embrace the positive effect they have on our sense of purpose, but the roles I play were affected in an unexpected way when I developed alopecia and suddenly went bald. I had no idea that losing my hair would create such an intense shift in all those relationships; and on their corresponding impact on my sense of who I am. Of course, alopecia has affected my identity – it seems too obvious to be worth saying – but I had no idea it would affect my identity *in this way*.

Here's an example of what I mean: losing my hair didn't change the fact I was a mother, but the *kind of mother* I was changed suddenly. I had always been a strong and decisive mum; but now I felt fragile and uncertain. I remember so clearly the moment in which I showed my ever-increasing bald patch to my eight-year-old twins, Jacob and Layla. I knew I couldn't hide it under ponytails for much longer and that they'd have to see it soon: I'd told them about it, but seeing my naked scalp with their own eyes was still a shock. Layla exclaimed, "You didn't tell us it was that bad!" and Jacob began to cry. Despite my own dark, sad, frightening feelings I comforted them. I told them it was only hair; that I'd still be beautiful; that I was still the same Mum I'd always been – all the platitudes that had been offered to me but which I knew wouldn't be helpful to my children any more than they had been to me. And I was right: the words were meaningless and despite all my efforts to keep smiling, Jacob and Layla could see

I was struggling. They saw me sobbing when someone let slip to the mums in the playground that my hair had fallen out; sharing my private ordeal before I was ready to. They saw me refuse to go outside to empty the bins without a hat on. They saw me nervously venturing out in my new wig, constantly tugging the back down and adjusting the fringe, asking for reassurance that I looked OK. My identity role as a mum had changed. My babies saw me as vulnerable and scared, and it was an identity shift that saddened me.

At the same time my identity as a wife was changing. Luke and I had only been married for a few months when my hair first started falling out, but in the four years we'd known each other he had always made me feel desirable, sexy and confident – in a way that no-one else had ever done. He helped me to see myself through his eyes, and I could feel myself glowing with self-belief when I viewed myself through the lens of my husband's unconditional adoration. But alopecia threatened all of that: I went from believing I was a "because" wife (he fancies me *because* I'm sexy; he wants me *because* I'm beautiful; he chose me *because* I'm valued) to envisaging myself as a "despite" wife (he still wants me *despite* me being bald, sad and unattractive). That was a deeply painful identity shift – "because" to "despite". It wasn't real, of course, as far as Luke was concerned. But it felt very real to me and it caused a physical pain in my gut to imagine how badly I'd let my gorgeous husband down by daring to become repulsive only months after he'd married me.

And my identity as a friend, always such an important part of who I was, was changing too: beyond all recognition. I hadn't told many friends what I was going through but those I did confide in saw a side of me that scares me even now. My thoughts were dark and frightening, seen by only a small number of my closest girlfriends. And although those friends and I had all supported each other through difficult times over the years, none of us had ever expressed such despair – such utter hopelessness – and been so completely inconsolable. I'd always seen myself as the funny friend; the friend who gave great advice; the friend who could be impulsive and spontaneous whilst also being the one who offered balanced and rational opinions. Those aspects of my identity as a friend had been completely lost, though, and being the needy, despondent one for the first time felt unfamiliar and frightening.

Other relationship roles changed too: with my parents and my brother; with colleagues in the schools I visited as a freelance educator; even with the teachers and other parents at Jacob and Layla's school. So, in the blink of an eye, the roles I saw myself playing in other people's lives changed. I went from *strong* mum to *vulnerable* mum; from a *desirable* wife to an *embarrassing* wife; from a *fun and supportive* friend to a *miserable and needy* one. And when you remember that those roles had, over the years, become the sum of my entire identity? *It meant I went from defining myself as strong, desirable, fun and supportive to vulnerable, embarrassing, miserable and needy.* All because my hair was falling out.

I had fallen victim to a scenario that I now know to be true for so many other women: I had tried to become all things to all people but had forgotten to be something to myself too. And so, when I lost those parts of my identity that were all about others, I lost any sense of who I was.

That story, in one form or another, is one I have helped countless women navigate as a coach. Almost without realising it, their lives have become consumed with managing and caring for others. Jess, for example, came to me for coaching telling me she was desperate to boost her self-esteem. She felt she had lost herself. Jess shared a very vivid and emotional metaphor in which she was made of brightly-coloured building bricks, each brick representing her identity in relation to others. One brick was stamped with the word "mother", another with "wife". Other bricks carried the labels "daughter" and "sister". There was a brick representing her job as an admin assistant; one was her role as the housewife; and one symbolised the responsibilities she felt towards her friends. Jess described being terrified that those building bricks – those identity roles – had become the sum total of who she was.

But when Jess and I explored the life she dreamed of living – one in which she was self-assured and confident in her own abilities – she shook her head and told me it could never happen. She knew that creating confidence, for example, would involve completely changing the shape and size of her "wife" brick, and Jess didn't know how she could do this without making her construction collapse. She knew also that her dream life would mean creating more time and space for herself, but that this would mean making the "friend" brick much, much smaller. Again, she wondered, how was this possible without damaging the entire structure?

You may or may not be able to relate to the imagery of the brick wall, but I can be certain that the list of roles that felt so confining to Jess (and to me) is something that will resonate with you. As a coach I hear about lives that revolve around being there for friends in need of advice; driving kids to after-school clubs; organising husbands' diaries; checking on ageing parents; supporting colleagues. Part of being a woman, it seems, is the overwhelming responsibility to be all things to all people. As children we are egocentric but, as we reach adulthood, relationships, motherhood... we feel a new sense of responsibility to those around us. For some women their experience is different, of course, but by and large this is the way the story goes.

But why does this happen? How do we end up being completely defined by our role in relation to others? There are many complex reasons for this, but one that comes up frequently is the need for approval. The outdated wisdom that girls should be made of "sugar and spice and all things nice" is still deeply rooted for many of us: to be seen as "all things nice" often feels like a pressure that can be overwhelming. So much of my work as a coach is helping women to see that having other people like them and approve of them *is not* the most important thing. It's worth asking yourself the question: "Am I playing these roles for others because it's what I *want* to do, or is it because I'm scared of how I'll be judged if I don't?"

If the fear of negative judgement is pushing you to say "yes" to everyone, it's time to do something about that. You don't need to feel bad for being this way. It's not your fault: it's come from a lifetime of messages – both obvious and subconscious – telling you that this is what "good girls" do. They're nice. They're kind. They say yes. They put everyone else before them.

But I learned the hard way that this mindset comes at a cost. Because when you build your entire identity around this (*"Like me!! Please, please like me!"*) you lose yourself in the process. Being there for others *can* be important: it can be gratifying to know that we play a valuable role in people's lives and to help those we care about; and it can serve to increase our sense of purpose. But when we allow that to eclipse everything else – when we allow our entire identity to be defined by who we are to others – that's when everything can fall apart as it did for me; or that is when you can end up feeling trapped like Jess did.

"Tell me about yourself".

I asked you earlier, but now I'm asking you again. And this time you'll need to dig deeper. Tell me about who you are as a person: your passions, your strengths, your dreams. You've discovered that when you tell someone about yourself you are likely to tell them about your family or your job. But that's not *you*. You are not your job or your partner or your children. We all have countless roles we play in our lives; but when you strip them all away... who's left? Who is the woman behind all the roles?

Guided Reflection 7:

Go back to your drawing in your notebook – the woman representing you, surrounded by the roles you play in people's lives. Inside the outline of the body write words that describe who you are. Not "who you are to others". Just who you are. Here's an example of how my own picture looks:

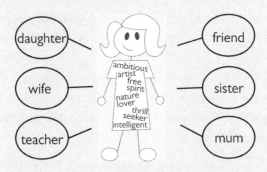

This is harder: it might even feel uncomfortable. It may help if you close your eyes and picture some of the times you've been truly happy; or picture your dreams and goals.

I know that you probably found this part of the Guided Reflection much more difficult than the first part, and I'd like to encourage you to ask yourself why. Could it be because you have been conditioned to believe that as a woman the most important thing for you to do is prioritise everyone else? It can be upsetting when you realise how much you have neglected your own happiness in favour of everyone else's; especially when you've done it to the point of almost forgetting who you are in your core. You may have started to believe that you are the sum of the roles you play in other people's lives, but as your Guided Reflection in this chapter shows, those roles do not define you. *You* define you. You haven't completely forgotten who you truly are when you strip away all the roles you play in other people's lives and it's not too late to reclaim those fundamental attributes that deserve your time and attention.

After all, it hasn't always been like this. When you were a child you knew who you were. You may not have known the names for every part of your essence, but you recognised them and honoured them instinctively. You weren't expected to be there for everyone else – in fact, others were expected to be there for you – and this gave you the freedom and the space to discover who you were. You could learn whether you loved adventure or if you were more risk-averse; whether you craved new experiences or preferred familiarity. You explored your creativity; your relationship to the world around you; your darkest fears and your most longed-for dreams. When you were a child you knew you were beautiful, in the truest sense of the word. You had a beautiful connection to your heart; to your soul; to your spirit.

That beautiful bond with yourself waned as your responsibilities grew. It's inevitable, and it's not something you should feel bad about. But I want you to know… *it is still there*. Every time you feel that sense of overwhelm: when the kids need to be picked up from a club, or your partner is demanding to know where he

"When you were a child
you knew you were beautiful,

in the truest sense of the word."

left his favourite socks; when your mum wants to know when you'll next visit, or your best friend is asking for time to dissect her latest dating disaster; when you want to scream: "*STOP! I can't be everything to everyone any more!*"… that's when you need to stop and listen. Because that almost-forgotten part of yourself that used to be so happy – that used to *know you* so well – is whispering… "*What about me?*" She wants you to rekindle that beautiful connection to your own heart. She wants you to carry on being there for those you care about – because this is important to you – but to also be there for *you* too.

Take another look at your drawing from your Guided Reflection. The roles you fulfil for others are important. But I want to remind you that you don't need to be all things to all people – in fact, no matter how hard you try you simply cannot. You can be *some* things to *some* people, though, and it is up to you to choose *which* things and *which* people. You can shape the roles you play in people's lives instead of feeling as though the roles have already been created without you having any say over how they look. You can still be there for those you care about – indeed, you should be – but it can be on your own terms so that you can determine how you'll prioritise your time and your energy. Your drawing shows you that your roles *are not you*. *You* are the words *inside* your drawing. And they're where to redirect your focus to help you reawaken all that is beautiful in you.

It's possible, my lovely. I promise you, it's possible.

Because after all, I no longer define myself as the vulnerable mum, the embarrassing wife, the miserable and needy friend. And I changed that in exactly the way I've described: I realised that I would continue to play important roles in the lives of others, but that I wanted to reconnect with my own sense of self, which had got lost along the way. I listened to the little, knowing voice inside, whispering to me that I love to write. I listened to her telling me that I wanted to spend time learning to do my make-up. I listened when she reminded me that I love singing, watching plays, and being near the sea. *I listened.* And the more I listened to what I wanted from myself, the more I felt that beautiful bond with my own identity strengthening once more.

Have I surprised you?

This might not have been what you expected when you first started reading a book called *How to Feel Beautiful*. Maybe you'd imagined we'd be focusing solely on external factors: but this is really important work. It may sound somewhat trite, but feeling beautiful really does start from within. It begins by noticing and fully acknowledging all those beautiful parts of your identity that have been lost and buried under an avalanche of responsibilities. And it involves reconnecting to that deep, intrinsic *knowing* that you were able to enjoy as a child, when you didn't question whether you deserve to be a priority.

Guided Reflection 8:

Tell me about yourself.

And do it fully, with an open heart. Write a paragraph (or a page… or a book…) saying exactly who you are. Who you are in your very core. Start with "I am…. (your name)" and continue from there.

- What makes your heart happy?
- What place feels like your true home?
- Which deepest dreams and desires lurk in your mind?
- What fears keep you awake at night?
- What parts of your personality are the key to knowing you?
- What do you love about yourself?

Give yourself permission to be brave with your language; even though I know there are words that might feel unfamiliar or which you're not sure whether it's OK to use about yourself. Do you feel, deep down, like you're strong and courageous? Fierce? Sensual? Inspiring? Spiritual? Remember that this notebook is for you alone: nobody else is here to pass judgement on the words you use to describe yourself. So, do this without limits.

Write it all down. Take your time over this. Do yourself justice – you deserve to have your true self expressed fully and completely.

Let me tell you about myself.

I am Lizi. I am beautiful. I am strong, desirable, fun and supportive. I am *not* all things to all people, but I am *some* things to *some* people. I have chosen which people I want to be something to, and I have chosen which things I want to be to them. I am not all things to all people, but I *am* all things to myself. I listen to my heart and I respond with kindness and with action; prioritising my own happiness and emotional wellbeing. I have given myself the time and space to see that I am beautiful regardless of my relationships with others. I am beautiful.

CHAPTER 6

New Habits, New You

By now you're probably itching to start creating the new you. I know there might be part of you that is questioning where this book is going: you started reading because you want to know how to feel beautiful and maybe you feel you're no closer. But another part of you – a bigger part of you – knows that you were never going to achieve such a profound transformation without exploring some deep and fundamental questions about how you see yourself and your place in the world.

Everything we've done together so far has been about laying the foundations for success. Acknowledging the narratives that have fed your self-image; scrutinising your goals and desires; and understanding who you are to your core were all important processes to work through. I want to take a minute to thank you for trusting me over the last five chapters and working through the Guided Reflections, even though you will have found them challenging and despite the fact you may have questioned the reasons for doing them. You are now at a point where you are ready to start making real, tangible changes. So, let's get to work.

First of all, I'm going to ask you to think about your unhelpful habits. I'm not talking about the "bad habits" you might traditionally think of: biting your nails, for example, or drinking too much caffeine. I'm talking about the habits that stop you from being the person you wrote about at the end of Chapter 5 in your last Guided Reflection; and the habits that are in the way of you achieving the True Goal you wrote about in Chapters 3 and 4.

We *all* have habits that stand in the way of our success and happiness. For example, my habit of comparing myself to other women is something I have to regularly work on keeping at bay. Until not very long ago I would do it without even noticing; appraising myself against every woman I saw. Which of us was fatter? Prettier? More fashionable? Who had applied their make up better? Who had straighter teeth or smoother skin? Who walked with more confidence? Of course, usually I found myself lacking; but even on the rare occasion that I "won" the comparison, it was a worthless victory that left me feeling like my physical appearance determined my entire value. Eventually I understood that unhelpful habits like this one were having a detrimental effect on my dreams and goals. And so, I worked on changing them.

Guided Reflection 9:

Thinking about your goals, reflect on the unhelpful habits you have developed that are going to stop you achieving your True Goal. Divide your page into four equal columns and at the top of the first one write the heading: "My unhelpful habits". Write down as many as you can think of.

You might want to think about the habits you have developed around:

- How you spend your time
  - For example, do you have a habit of sitting in front of the TV while the kids are at school, or scrolling through social media when you'd planned to work?
- How you speak to yourself
  - For example, do you have a habit of telling yourself you're lazy, stupid or a failure if you fall short of your goals? Do you tell yourself you're not enough?
- How you speak about yourself
  - For example, do you have a habit of putting yourself down in front of others? Do you make self-deprecating jokes to hide your insecurities?
- How you treat your body
  - For example, do you have a habit of eating crisps and chocolate when you're in the car? Do you drink more alcohol than you'd like to?

- How you respond to being asked for your time and energy
  - For example, do you have a habit of saying yes to everyone even when you don't want to? Do you exhaust yourself doing things for others?

Once you've done this, in the second column write the heading "The Negative Effects". Next to each habit you've written, write how it affects your ability to achieve your goals, and the effect it has on your state of mind and emotional wellbeing. For example, here's what my client Fiona said when I worked through this exercise with her:

My Unhelpful Habits	The Negative Effects		
I have a habit of coming home from the morning school run and sitting in front of the TV with a cup of tea and some biscuits. I end up staying there for a couple of hours.	Wasting that time makes me feel bad. By lunchtime I feel guilty that I didn't do something more productive and then I get super-critical with myself.		

Leave your last two columns empty for now – we'll come back to them soon.

Identifying the habits is the easy part (*I know, I know… that wasn't easy at all!*). The hard part is changing them. But I did it and you can too. The key is to replace an old habit with a new one, rather than just attempting to stop the old one… and that's because your current habits exist to fulfil a need. It might be the need to reduce boredom; to satisfy a food craving; to avoid being judged adversely by others; to distract yourself from negative or damaging thoughts. If you try to simply remove the habit (going "cold turkey") the need will still be there and you'll end up returning to the habit you're trying to drop, so we have to get really clear on what that need actually is. The next step, then, is for you to go back to the unhelpful habits you've identified and work out what need they are fulfilling.

Guided Reflection 10:

Return to your list of unhelpful habits and the negative effects they have on your life. In the third column write the heading "The Fulfilled Need", and for each habit write down what you get out of engaging in that habit. Think beyond the obvious, immediate answers and ask yourself what emotional need is being met. This part of the work might feel tough; it involves digging deep and you may uncover some needs you didn't know were lurking. Give yourself enough time and space to think this through properly. For example, this is what my client Fiona discovered about her needs:

My Unhelpful Habits	The Negative Effects	The Fulfilled Need	
I have a habit of coming home from the morning school run and sitting in front of the TV with a cup of tea and some biscuits. I end up staying there for a couple of hours.	Wasting that time makes me feel bad. By lunchtime I feel guilty that I didn't do something more productive and then I get super-critical with myself.	The morning routine is stressful and getting home to a peaceful house is a big relief. I have a need to do something quiet and restful, that's just for me. My sofa time feels like a decadent treat that I've earned.	

The final stage of this exercise is really important and it's why you might have struggled to break unhelpful habits in the past. You take the habit away and feel virtuous… but the need is still there. And so, you either feel unhappy because you now have an unfulfilled emotional need; or you return to the old habit because the need is too strong to ignore. To avoid falling back into that same pattern, one of two things needs to happen. Your first option is to find a new, alternative habit that fulfils the need but without the negative effects. And the second option is to think about how you can remove the need all together (or at least reduce it significantly) so that you don't need a habit to fulfil it at all. This is going to take some work now, but I promise it's worth it.

Guided Reflection 11:

In your final column write the heading: "My Plan". And then for each row decide whether you can find a way to remove or reduce the need, or whether you want to replace the habit with a different, more positive one. And then decide on a plan. For example:

My Unhelpful Habits	The Negative Effects	The Fulfilled Need	My Plan
I have a habit of coming home from the morning school run and sitting in front of the TV with a cup of tea and some biscuits. I end up staying there for a couple of hours.	Wasting that time makes me feel bad. By lunchtime I feel guilty that I didn't do something more productive and then I get super-critical with myself.	The morning routine is stressful and getting home to a peaceful house is a big relief. I have a need to do something quiet and restful, that's just for me. My sofa time feels like a decadent treat that I've earned.	EITHER – Plan a new, positive habit: When I get home from the school run, I'll do a ten-minute meditation and keep a daily gratitude journal. This will create special quiet time that sets me up for a productive day. OR – Remove/reduce the need: I will make the morning routine less stressful by getting the kids to help prepare for it the night before. Then I won't feel the need to recover when I get home from school in the morning.

Fiona and I identified a way for her to create a new habit, and we also looked at a way for her to reduce the need. She felt that she wouldn't be able to reduce the need enough to make a meaningful difference, but decided she loved the sound of the new habit we'd thought of, and so this is what she chose to work on with me.

Well done. That's a lot of work I've just asked you to do. How does it feel now, to see your habits written down and to know there *is* an alternative? You have just proved to yourself that you *can* leave the unhelpful, negative habits behind and create new habits that feed into achieving your True Goal.

We're going to move on now to think about exactly *how* you can start integrating your fourth column into your life. The first thing for you to know about changing your habits is that psychologists all agree: successful change follows a process. It can't "just happen". Take Fiona's example which I shared in the Guided Reflections. She decided to change her habits when she got home from the school run: she wanted to stop sitting in front of the TV for hours and start meditating and gratitude journaling instead. She was actually feeling really enthusiastic in our session and ready to immediately cast off her old habits and dive straight into her new morning routine. She was surprised when I stopped her. But Fiona was missing an important understanding: the difference between "change" and "transition". Change is situational. It's about Fiona buying a new notebook and sitting at the kitchen table instead of the sofa when she got home. Change is about *doing* things differently. Transition is the process of moving from the old you to the new you, and I knew I needed to support Fiona with the transition away from her old morning habit and into the new one. Transition is about Fiona following her new habits every morning without even having to think about it. It's about Fiona no longer feeling sad about saying goodbye to her mornings on the sofa, because she has fully integrated her new habits into her life. If change is about *doing*, transition is about *feeling*. And so, whilst Fiona was ready to change instantly, we had to spend time working on her transition too.

This, by the way, is why you might not have succeeded in the past when you've tried to change your habits. Maybe you've started a diet plan, for example, thrown away all the biscuits and started virtuously eating salad for lunch every day. But after a couple of weeks the old eating habits have crept back in. It's because you jumped straight into the change but didn't make the emotional transition from your old self to the new at the same time (as well as not understanding the emotional need your biscuit habit was fulfilling).

The best thing you can do to aid your transition is to break your new habit into a series of small changes and build up to the full transition. For example, Fiona decided that to start with she would commit to listening to her ten-minute meditation when she got home each morning, and would allow herself her "sofa time" after she'd done it. Once this became a comfortable new habit, Fiona introduced the next small change: writing her gratitude journal in between her meditation and her time on the sofa. Next, she put a timer on her TV viewing and planned a productive task to complete when she turned the TV off. And finally, once she had grown comfortable with all these small changes, she felt ready to give up her morning sofa and TV time all together. Her old, unhelpful habit was a thing of the past. The whole process took Fiona around a month to complete and by the end of the month her changes had resulted in a successful transition for her. That time frame is pretty typical: most psychologists agree that it takes between twenty and thirty days to develop a new habit.

So that's the first thing for you to know: change and transition are different, and it takes time to fully transition into a new version of you. Once you have fully integrated the new habits into your life they come easily, but while you're working on creating the transition it can be tough going at times. It might take all your willpower and self-control not to revert back to the old, unhelpful habits that you're trying to leave behind.

And this leads us to the second thing you need to know. I do understand that seeing that final column describing a long list of happy, positive habits might feel really tempting. You'd be forgiven for wanting to dive right in with five or six of them. But don't! Even making small, incremental changes like Fiona did involves using significant willpower and self-control at first. Many psychologists agree that our self-control isn't unlimited, and that if you overdo it you can end up suffering from a state known as ego depletion. This happens when you use up all your available willpower on one task, leaving you with little self-control to exercise in other areas (think of the dieter who uses all their self-control to follow their meal plans during the week and then loses control at the weekend). The danger is that if you try to make too many changes at once you may use up all your willpower on the first change, and then give yourself a hard time because you've been unable to maintain the self-control you need for the other changes you'd planned to tackle. So, go easy on yourself here and don't rush it. Choose one or two new positive habits from your list and work on those first. To help you choose which one(s) to start with, read through your True Goal again and consider which old habits are holding you back from achieving it. Which new habits from your last column will help you to get closer to your True Goal?

Guided Reflection 12:

It's time to make a commitment to yourself. Copy and complete these sentences:

- The first unhelpful habit I'm going to work on changing is…

- I've chosen this one to start with because...
- My plan is to... (*create a new habit of... or remove the need by...*)
- The first small changes I will make to achieve this are...
- I'm going to start this on/when...
- Once I've completed my transition from the old habit, I'll feel...
- This will bring me closer to my True Goal by...

If this feels a little confusing, have a look at Fiona's example:

- The first unhelpful habit I'm going to work on changing is sitting in front of the TV for two hours every morning.
- I've chosen this one to start with because if I can start my day being more mindful and productive it will have a positive effect on my work, home and state of mind.
- My plan is to replace the TV habit with meditating and gratitude journaling.
- The first small changes I will make to achieve this are downloading a meditation and listening to it as soon as I get home every morning.
- I'm going to start this when the new school term starts.
- Once I've completed my transition from the old habit, I'll feel proud of myself for using my time

productively. I'll feel able to achieve more during the day.
- This will bring me closer to my True Goal by giving me more hours in the day to work on my personal development, and increasing my self-esteem.

Your turn. Write down the commitment you're ready to make to yourself.

I'm going to finish this chapter by returning to my own story, and my unhelpful habit of comparing myself to other women. After a great deal of reflection, I understood the negative effect this was having on me. It was leaving me feeling objectified and believing that my physical appearance was the most important measure of my own value; and because I didn't rate my physical appearance very highly it meant my self-worth was dropping lower and lower. It was hard to uncover these realisations about myself, and I shed plenty of tears when I fully understood the impact of my self-inflicted habits.

I went on to explore the need I was fulfilling by engaging in this destructive habit. I discovered that it was all connected to my need to understand what I was *worth* – especially in other people's eyes. By continually moving myself up and down my own imaginary league table of women, I was fulfilling my need to know where I fitted in, and my need to know what others must think about me. This work was difficult for me, and it might be for you too. Unpicking your own thinking like this can uncover some challenging truths.

But I persevered and worked through it, and like you've just done I thought about whether I wanted to create a new habit or reduce the need that was feeding the habit. For me, reducing that need felt really important. I didn't want to feel reliant on other people's opinions of me (or the opinions I *imagined* they had) and I didn't want to keep believing that my appearance determined my worth. I didn't want to keep creating lists of women who outstripped me in their appearance.

I began working on a new list: a list of people whose opinions about me *mattered*. And then I started thinking about what attributes they valued in me. I wrote it all down... and I realised that most of them couldn't care less what I looked like. They cared whether I was kind or funny, they cared that I was a good mum, they cared that I was generous with my time, that I was ambitious and intelligent, that I was a good listener. And bit by bit, I dropped the unhelpful habit. I stopped comparing myself to other women. I started to recognise what was beautiful about me, and almost without trying I developed a new habit of speaking kindly *about* myself and *to* myself.

We've done loads of work in this chapter – you must be exhausted! Don't panic if you're feeling a bit overwhelmed by it all. You might be thinking, "This is all very well *in theory*, but in reality how will I ever find the motivation to get started and to persevere with

"They cared whether I was kind or funny,
they cared that I was a good mum,

they cared that I was generous
with my time…"

this?" Well, you're in luck! The next chapter is all about motivation and it's going to leave you feeling more motivated than Cinderella trying to get home before the clock chimed twelve! That coffee (or merlot!) that I suggested you pour five chapters ago must be long gone. Go and get a refill for your mug or wine glass and get ready for some motivation to help you make those new habits a reality, and to bring your True Goal within touching distance.

CHAPTER 7

Let's Get Motivated!

I once asked on social media: "What's the main thing you'd like to know about motivation?" The response was unanimous: "*How to get more of it!*" It's easy to feel unmotivated. It's human nature to know what we *should* be doing whilst finding ourselves procrastinating, wasting time, and telling ourselves we will *definitely, definitely* do it tomorrow.

And maybe you're concerned that a lack of motivation is going to stop you from moving forward with the exciting, beautiful plans you've put into place over the last few chapters to reach your True Goal. You're probably (hopefully!) feeling enthusiastic and excited right now, while it's all still feeling fresh and new. Your motivation levels are likely to be pretty high. But we all know that it's impossible to maintain that level of motivation forever, and that whilst you'll start working on your goals with positive intentions there's every chance that over time your motivation levels will start to drop off and those unhelpful habits you've worked so hard to shake off may start looking tempting again.

Guided Reflection 13:

How do you usually try to motivate yourself when something needs to be done?

- Do you promise yourself a treat when it's finished?
- Do you tell yourself off for not doing it?
- Do you threaten yourself with the consequences of ignoring it?
- Do you tell someone else your plans to make yourself accountable?
- Do you remind yourself of times you've done it before?
- Do you tell yourself you'll share your achievement afterwards?
- Do you give yourself a deadline to complete it?
- Do you break it down into smaller steps?

Try to think of some concrete examples of times you've tried to motivate yourself to get something done and, in your notebook, write what techniques you used.

There's every chance that you've just discovered that you use methods to try to motivate yourself without even realising that was what you were doing. But I'm also going to guess that a lot of the time you haven't actually thought about whether those motivational techniques really work. And you probably haven't stopped to ask yourself whether they work *for you*. What works for your best friend, your sister or your mum might not be motivating for you at all.

That's why I'm going to be sharing with you one of my favourite parts of my coaching process now! It's time to learn about exactly how *you* are motivated and how you can use that knowledge to ensure you succeed in reaching your True Goal. But what do we even mean by "motivation"? I know that for the women I work with as their coach, feeling motivated means feeling committed to an action, and feeling like they can tackle it. It means they won't find reasons to avoid it; and that even if it's difficult – or something they don't really want to do – they'll do it anyway.

Guided Reflection 14:

Think of some times you felt highly motivated.

Your examples might be from important and significant times in your life, but equally they might be small moments from your day-to-day life. If you're feeling a bit short on ideas it might help you to know some of the examples my clients have given when I've asked them the same question:

- "I felt motivated to stick to my diet in the months before my wedding".

- "I felt motivated to create a brilliant presentation for my team at work".
- "I felt motivated to find a new job after I was made redundant".
- "I felt motivated to tidy when my mum phoned to say she'd be round in an hour".
- "I felt motivated to study for my exams to make my children proud of me".
- "I felt motivated to ask for a pay rise when I learned my colleague earns more than me".

It's your turn. Try to recall some times when you felt high in energy and willpower and felt able to stick to your plan to get something done, and write them down.

As a qualified coach, I have studied the psychology of motivation *a lot*. It's an area that fascinates me. There are so many different theories about what "motivation" is, how to increase it, and whether it even exists. But there was one idea I read that really resonated with me above anything else, and which I have gone on to develop further into my own unique way of exploring your motivation. In his book *The Motivation Breakthrough*★, American educationist Richard Lavoie talks about the Six Ps of motivation. He identified six different ways for teachers to motivate their students depending on the type of child and the way they are best motivated:

79

through *power, prestige, prizes, praise, people* or *projects*. I realised that these principles could be applied to the women I worked with, but that those six motivators didn't quite cover everything. So, I added three more of my own to incorporate my own experience as a coach and some other psychological theories of motivation: my extra three Ps being *pride, punishment* and *pressure*.

Working through my motivation analysis has been a pivotal experience for many of my clients. Sarah, for example, came to me feeling frustrated that she couldn't stay motivated to stick to an exercise plan. She knew from our work together that her ultimate aim of feeling beautiful and confident would come from being fit and strong. She devised an exercise plan that she felt enthusiastic about at first, but after a few weeks her motivation had dropped. She asked me what she was doing wrong. She was acutely aware that her father had sadly passed away from a heart attack in his fifties, and she was scared that, if she didn't increase her fitness, she would be risking the same fate. Sarah tearfully said to me one day: "I'm telling myself every day that if I don't get fit I could die. I *know* that my children will have to grow up without me, and they'll blame me for letting them down. If this isn't motivating me, what the hell will?"

So, I worked through my motivation analysis with Sarah and we discovered that she was most likely to be motivated by *pride* and *prestige* (don't worry, I'll explain this all shortly). Yet she'd been *trying* to motivate herself with the threat of *punishment*. She'd been telling herself about all the awful things that would happen if she didn't achieve her goals, and then feeling despondent that these fears didn't motivate her. Once we worked out that she needed to change her tactics Sarah used her new-found understanding to enter herself into a half-marathon. She pictured herself crossing the finish line and collecting her medal. Together we created a strong and powerful visualisation of that moment and how it would feel to her. *That* method worked because Sarah was motivated by *pride* and *prestige*, so working towards both of those drivers meant she felt motivated to train for her big event. We also found that Sarah was motivated by *people,* so she leveraged that knowledge and joined a local weekly parkrun and started going to the gym regularly. It wasn't long before she began to see the results she'd been hoping for. Sarah's fitness levels soared, as did her confidence and self-belief. And all because we'd explored Sarah's motivation in a way she'd never considered before. Training for a half-marathon motivated Sarah infinitely more than regularly threatening herself with a heart attack.

Not only that, but the people closest to her who'd been trying to help had actually been having the opposite effect! Sarah's husband, for example, had offered to take her out and buy her some new clothes if she dropped a clothes size as a result of her fitness efforts. To him this was highly motivating. Sarah's husband (she later realised) was most motivated by *prizes*, and so because this was the type of motivation he understood best he thought that, by offering his wife a tangible reward for her efforts, he was being supportive and encouraging. The actual effect though was to make Sarah resentful of his offer: for her it wasn't motivating but instead meant that her husband was loading unnecessary pressure on her.

Once Sarah understood that *pride* and *prestige* were the most important motivators to her she was able to think about ways her husband could use those to meaningfully support her in a way that would actually be helpful.

Guided Reflection 15:

Use my motivation wheel to discover where your motivation comes from. For each of the nine Ps, ask yourself how much it drives you to carry through with an action or plan without making excuses or finding reasons to avoid it. How much is each P going to persuade you to stick with it, even when it's tricky?

Start at the top with "praise" and see if you can think of a time you've received praise (or had the potential to receive it). Did it help to spur you on? Write "praise" in your notebook and give it a score out of 10; the higher the score the more motivating it is for you. Then move on to the next P-word and carry on around the circle. Don't forget to think about Guided Reflection 11 and the times you remember being highly motivated, and ask yourself which of the Ps were at play then (it might have been more than one). For example, if you were motivated to tidy when your mum was due to come round, were you feeling motivated by the pressure to do it quickly? The threat of punishment if your mum was likely to be critical? Or maybe the potential for praise if she was likely to comment on your clean house?

Now you should have in your notebook one or more motivational drivers that have the highest numbers, and this is powerful information! Look back at Guided Reflection 10 and the ways you've been trying to motivate yourself up until now. How often have you been using the right Ps for you, and how many times have you frustrated yourself, like Sarah did, by trying to motivate yourself in completely the wrong way?

So now you have this incredible insight into the way you work, let's think about how you can use it. Back in Guided Reflection 3 you created your very own True Goal. And in Guided Reflection 12 you made a plan of the steps you need to take to achieve that goal. Next, you're going to ramp up your motivation to help you succeed in changing those habits for good, just like Sarah did when she incorporated her new-found knowledge by joining a local parkrun and signing up for a half-marathon.

Another client, Lisa, discovered she was most motivated by *praise*. So, she leveraged this by keeping a "praise journal" on her at all times: a notebook in which she wrote down the positive things people said to her. Whenever she doubted her ability to see her plan through, she took out the notebook and read all the lovely ways people had praised her. She found it highly motivating and this little notebook was the key to succeeding in her plans.

Guided Reflection 16:

How can you use your top motivators to help you reach your True Goal more easily? You are allowed to engineer situations and ask people for exactly what you want. I know you might not be used to that, but I'm giving you permission. So, with that in mind, here are some ideas. You'll have lots more of your own.

- If you're most motivated by *praise* can you keep a notebook like Lisa did? Can you ask family and friends to let you know if they think you're doing well?
- If you're most motivated by *prestige* can you share your accomplishments publicly – on social media or even in the local press – to show what you've achieved?
- If you're most motivated by *punishment* can you find a picture of the situation you most want to avoid and stick it somewhere you'll see often?
- If you're most motivated by *people* is there a team or club you can join that is working towards a similar goal as you?
- If you're most motivated by *prizes* can you promise yourself a treat when you reach milestones? Can you ask your parents or partner to treat you?
- If you're most motivated by *pride* can you keep a journal to capture the amazing feeling of

achievement each time you reach another small step?

- If you're most motivated by *projects* can you break your goal down into defined steps with a measurable completion point for each one?
- If you're most motivated by *pressure* can you set yourself a deadline and ask someone you trust to hold you accountable to it?
- If you're most motivated by *power* can you take charge of (or set up) a team working towards the same goal as you?

There are so many ways you can apply your own top motivators to your goals with a little creative thinking. So, looking at the plan you committed to in Guided Reflection 9, write down now how you will motivate yourself to stick to the plan and carry through on all the actions you're intending to work on.

I've always known I was highly motivated by *praise*, and I used this (subconsciously at the time) to help me achieve my goal of not comparing myself to other women any more. I began to own my identity as a bald woman and started sharing photos of my true self on social media; of course, the praise came flooding in. Friends telling me I was beautiful. Strangers telling me I was brave. Clients telling me I was inspirational. And the more I received these positive comments, the more

I was encouraged to keep seeing myself the way I *wanted* to see myself. Every time I was given some praise, I felt a little more motivated to keep going. I know now that it's what stopped me from slipping back into my old destructive habits of comparing myself to other women; and encouraged me to keep seeing the beauty in myself until it became a new habit that I didn't even have to *try* to do any more.

And now you're ready to do the same. You know what you want to do and how it will help you to achieve your beautiful True Goal. And you know how to motivate

yourself to do it! Well done, my lovely. With every chapter, and every Guided Reflection, you're getting to know yourself better. I promised you at the start of this book that by the time you reached the end you would be a slightly different woman. Can you feel that starting to happen? Have you ever before *fully* understood what you want and why you want it? Have you ever *truly* known what steps you need to take to feel beautiful, confident and motivated? You're changing, my darling. You're learning how to feel beautiful. Your transformation is well under way, and I am so very proud.

★ Lavoie, R. (2008) *The Motivation Breakthrough*, Atria Books: New York.

CHAPTER 8

Supporters and Saboteurs

No man – or woman – is an island. Having support from those around you can be the key to succeeding, and equally a lack of support can mean your plans dissolve in an instant – no matter how committed or motivated you are. When I decided I wanted to train to be a coach, for example, I asked my husband, Luke, for his opinion. He said he thought I'd be a brilliant coach and that I should go for it. So, I did. If he'd laughed at me or told me it was a bad idea there's every chance I'd have given up on it.

Some people *don't* give up in the face of opposition, of course: you might be someone who thinks "I'll show them!" and who doubles down on your efforts. Maybe you even find it strongly motivating. But even then, this changes your mindset. It feels different to be working towards a goal knowing you've got a team of supporters cheering you on, than it does to be working on it to prove your doubters wrong. It's so much better to be working on a project carried along on a wave of positivity: it energises you and boosts you when you need it. When you're trying to achieve something in the face of negativity it's draining. You can't focus your whole emotional energy on your goal because you end up apportioning some of it to your nay-sayers.

Take Carrie, for example. When she started her coaching journey with me, she was feeling overwhelmed and unappreciated. She had a part-time job as a reflexologist, and outside of this was still expected to be the family's cook, cleaner, taxi driver, social secretary, administrator and general dogsbody. So, Carrie decided to create a large planner to put on the kitchen wall, listing all the tasks that needed to be done to keep the family running smoothly and dividing them fairly between herself, her husband and their two children. At a coaching session with me, Carrie said she wanted to ask her husband to help write the schedule with her, but she was nervous that he would think the idea was ridiculous. She told me she was scared she'd give up on it too quickly if he dismissed it as silly, and was worried that she'd end up feeling even worse about her situation if she ended up trying to get her children to carry out chores without her husband's backing.

A week later, Carrie came to her next session feeling euphoric. Her husband had told her the wall planner was an excellent idea, and had helped her to implement it by taking on his share of the household work whilst also backing Carrie up in their new expectations of the children. His support gave Carrie the strength she needed to see her plan through, and to believe it was worth doing.

And the same will be true for you, my lovely. As you begin working towards your True Goal there are people who will support you and people who will sabotage you. Knowing how to leverage your supporters whilst distancing your saboteurs will make your journey towards your goal a happier one. More than that, in fact, it will help you to achieve your goal. After all, psychologists agree that the more strongly you believe in your ability to succeed at something the more likely you are to actually do it… and I'm sure you know that when you've got people in your corner cheering you on, your self-belief rockets.

Guided Reflection 17:

Identify all your supporters and write them in your notebook. Think beyond the obvious and include anyone who you think might be an ally in your journey towards your True Goal. Remember that "support" can take many forms: it could be emotional support, practical support, financial support, professional support, spiritual support… or other types of support that you might feel you need.

- Start by thinking about your household. Is there anyone who has your back, no matter what?
- Expand your thinking to extended family and your friendship circle. Who can you rely on to step up when you ask them to?

- Do you have supporters you've never met in real life? We live in an age where Facebook friends can be the most ardent, non-judgmental supporters we have.
- Can you think of a time when someone has instinctively known what help you've needed and offered it without waiting to be asked?
- Now turn your thoughts to professionals you can ask for help. Do you know of coaches, counsellors, teachers, trainers, mentors or doctors who might be able to support you in your journey?
- Feel free to add me to your list! I've supported countless women working towards their goals and I am here to support you too. You'll find ways to contact me at the end of this book.

In the difficult weeks following the onset of my alopecia I had a great deal of support – and it was very much needed, since my belief that I could ever feel beautiful again was non-existent. Friends and family showed me encouragement and thoughtfulness, which helped me a great deal. I hadn't thought about creating a concrete goal at that time, but if I had done, it would have been to come to terms with my hair loss and accept it as part of me. Some friends bought me gifts: pretty headscarves, books and flowers. Others showed their support with words: telling me I would still be beautiful; telling me they were sorry this was happening to me. Some reminded me that I was strong: that I'd got through worse and I'd get through this.

The cumulative effect of so many little gestures was one of making me feel nurtured and *held*. And my best supporter – the one who met me *right where I was* – and instinctively offered up exactly what I needed, was my daughter Layla.

She was eight when I went bald. I had tried so hard to be brave for her and her twin brother Jacob. I'd tried so hard not to let them see me cry. I'd smiled and told them their mum would be beautiful no matter what, hoping they couldn't hear my heart hammering in my chest as I said it. But one day Layla asked me if I was sad about my hair falling out and I said yes, I was. She replied: "I'm not surprised you're sad. I'd be sad too." And *that* was what I had needed to hear. More than anything else I'd needed to be acknowledged in those clear, simple terms. I had needed someone to tell me my feelings were right and valid. And whilst I am certain I'd had other supporters who had said versions of the same thing, it was Layla who had found the *precise* support I had needed to help me move forward. I cried at her words and she cuddled me and told me everything would be all right… and I believed her.

Of course, the very best supporters you can hope for are the ones who instinctively know what you need from them to help you towards your goal, and who offer it up unquestioningly – like Layla did for me. But the reality is, most of your supporters won't fall into this category. They are people with their own lives, their own struggles and challenges, who might not see that you need help. They are people with their own views about what *they* would find helpful and who will tend to offer that kind of help first. They are people who care about you but who are fallible and who get things wrong.

Even Luke, my wonderful, supportive husband – my soulmate – didn't quite give me the precise support I wanted from him when my hair was falling out. He reassured me day after day that no matter what happened he would still love me. But that wasn't what I wanted to hear from him: I *knew* my baldness wouldn't make him stop loving me. I was scared he'd stop *fancying* me. I wanted to know that he'd still *want me*, and *that's* what I needed to hear from him.

Guided Reflection 18:

Return to your list of supporters and think about what support you would like from each of them. It's important to get specific. For example, rather than writing "emotional support" you could write: "a weekly phone call to check how I'm doing" or "a hug when I'm feeling low".

I suggest writing it as a spider diagram or flow chat as that will help you with the next Guided Reflection. For example, one of my clients, Diana, identified her mum as one of her supporters, and wrote down different ways her mum could support her:

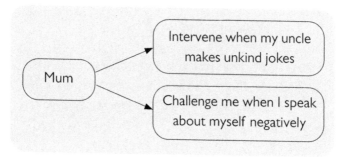

Back to my own story... and the whole time Luke was telling me he would love me no matter how much hair I had, I was allowing myself to become sad and frustrated that he wasn't giving me what I *wanted* from him: reassurance that he would still fancy me. But eventually I realised that he was doing his absolute best in supporting me and that I had to take some responsibility in asking for the support I needed. And so, I explained to Luke exactly what I needed from him to help me achieve my goal of becoming comfortable with my alopecia. It meant letting myself get vulnerable: it wasn't easy telling my gorgeous husband that I was scared he'd stop fancying me. But it was also empowering to explain what I needed to hear, to help me start making my peace with my hair loss. And of course, as my supporter, Luke immediately acted on what I'd asked of him and showed me how much he fancied me, at every available opportunity!

Guided Reflection 19:

The final part of your diagram involves you asking the question, "What is *my* part in this?" How can you take responsibility for getting the support you need to achieve your True Goal?

Going back to Diana's example, we discussed how she could get her mum to challenge her when she speaks about herself negatively. Diana suggested that the answer was to talk to her mum and I pushed her a little further, asking, "What will you say to her?" Getting specific was important again. So, in the end, Diana identified four different actions she could take to help her mum give her the kind of support she wanted:

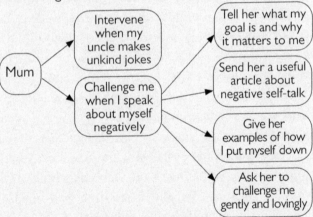

And, of course, Diana had identified many different supporters, just as you have done, and various ways she would like each of them to support her. So, by the time we had worked out Diana's part in gaining support from each of them she felt empowered, in control, and ready to ask for the support she needed to get to her True Goal.

So, you've got a plan now. You know who your supporters are (or who you would like them to be), what support you want from them, and what part you're going to play in getting the support you need. But what about your saboteurs? I know that no matter what your True Goal is there will be people who seem set on sabotaging it for you, and that sabotage can come in many forms. Often it involves putting you in the position of having to defend your goals. For example, one of my clients, Cathy, had decided to pursue her dream of pushing her fitness to a new level: she was lifting weights and building muscle, and loving the feeling of emotional and spiritual power that came with her new physical strength. But she was constantly being questioned by friends and family: "Don't you think you've done enough now?", "Aren't you worried you won't look feminine any more?" and even: "Doesn't your husband mind you spending so much time at the gym?" It felt to her like she was being undermined at every turn, and she was forever expending energy explaining why she wanted to achieve this goal. The sense of constantly having to justify herself and her goals was really starting to get Cathy down.

There's no doubt about it: once the saboteurs get hold of your goal you can find it slipping away from you. But you can tackle them head-on and make sure your goal doesn't end up falling by the wayside, and I'm going to show you how. I'd like to start by encouraging you to think about them in two categories: your accidental saboteurs and your deliberate saboteurs. Accidental saboteurs are people who do care about you but who sabotage things unintentionally. They'll say things like: "Are you sure you're not taking too much on?" or: "We're worried you're losing too much weight," or: "Will you still have enough time for the children?" The thing you need to remember about accidental saboteurs is that their intention isn't to upset you, and they do want you to be happy and successful: they just think they know better than you do how you should achieve that! They struggle to trust your own ability to know what's best for you. Keep reminding yourself that this isn't about you: it's about them, and their own issues and stories. And because they care about you, they want to "help".

Guided Reflection 20:

Make a list of your accidental saboteurs and write down:
- how they sabotage your goals
- how that makes you feel
- why they do it – from *their* perspective

This can feel counter-intuitive but it's a powerful task, so put your preconceptions to one side and give it a try.

Here's an example that Cathy worked through. She was feeling very despondent about the comments she was receiving about her fitness goals, particularly from her dad:

- Dad – sabotages my goals by joking that I look like a man now I'm building muscle.
- It makes me feel humiliated and like he doesn't respect me. It makes me feel like something that's really important to me feels like a joke to him. I feel like someone who loves me would be proud of me and happy to see me feeling positive, so it makes me feel like he doesn't love me when he does this.
- From Dad's perspective:
  "It makes me uncomfortable seeing Cathy changing like this. I believe women should look feminine and so Cathy's decisions aren't what I would choose for her. And I worry that other people will judge her too. I think of her as my little girl and I want other people to see her that way too."

Cathy got quite tearful writing this from her dad's perspective, and you might find it an emotional task too. But once you can imagine what your saboteur is thinking, it helps you to know how to tackle them.

Doing this work moved Cathy from the mindset of being angry and hurt by her dad's constant sabotage to feeling empowered and in control, and even a little sorry for him. She had a conversation with her dad acknowledging how her goals made him feel and explaining why they were so important to her. She told him that his support meant a great deal to her and that she would love it if he could be more understanding and show her some encouragement. Cathy's dad stopped teasing her and started telling her that he was proud of her hard work. He began complimenting her strength and dedication. In that one conversation, Cathy turned her accidental saboteur into a deliberate supporter. I would love you to plan some similar conversations after working through Guided Reflection 17. You have the power to transform accidental saboteurs into supporters too.

Finally, we need to think about your deliberate saboteurs. Hopefully they are few and far between, but sadly they do emerge from time to time, and their impact can be devastating. Think about my own goal to feel beautiful, and the saboteurs I told you about in Chapter 4. Steve, the boy at school who wrote me a letter telling me all the ways I needed to look different before he'd go out with me, for example, wasn't acting out of a misguided sense of wanting what was best for me. Steve was just a dick. Steve's priority was impressing his friends and he did it by belittling and humiliating me.

And then just three years later there were the friends

of my then-boyfriend Jack, who invented a new joke that I didn't understand. Whenever we were together, they would sing *"tree!"* to each other and collapse with laughter. I didn't know what was funny, but I'd laugh with them... until Jack eventually explained the joke. Once, I had gone clubbing with them all wearing a short skirt. The boys decided I had legs like tree trunks. The joke was *me*.

This was deliberate sabotage at its finest: I had already been acutely aware that my legs were chunky but had worn the short skirt anyway because I liked it. After discovering that my fat legs hadn't only been noticed but had become the subject of a mean joke, I never wore a short skirt again.

Of course, the best thing to do when someone deliberately and knowingly sabotages your beautiful goals is to walk away, but it's not always easy. When Steve, Rick, Jack's friends and my science teacher decided it was acceptable to crush my self-belief to make themselves feel good, I didn't know that I was allowed to reject them. But of course, I *was* allowed, and you are too. This is one of the reasons I believe it's so important to make time for self-care: because when you invest in yourself you are sending a message that you are worthy and valued, and subsequently you don't have to put up with anyone who doesn't see that. Self-care can take many forms, but one of the most powerful acts of self-care you can practice is surrounding yourself with your supporters and distancing yourself from deliberate saboteurs. They are not worth your energy.

Because of the work you've done over the last few Guided Reflections you now have a strong tribe of supporters, and you can use them when those deliberate saboteurs come your way. You've been practicing asking your supporters for the help you need, and you can ask them to step up and shield you when it's needed too. Let *them* deal with the saboteurs for you. Because, believe me, there's no-one more formidable than your strongest supporters fighting your corner.

"there's no-one more formidable than your strongest supporters fighting your corner"

You've done such important work in this chapter! Why not call one of your supporters to celebrate with you? Your wine glass probably needs topping up again: get a refill and then let's continue!

CHAPTER 9

What Is "Beautiful" Anyway?

We're eight chapters in now… and if you've been working through the Guided Reflections you should be much clearer on *why* feeling beautiful matters to you; *how* you're going to achieve it; and *who* you can rely on to help you get there. But there's one important question we haven't explored yet, which is this: What *is* "beautiful"?

For so many years my beliefs about what constituted a "beautiful woman" fell within some pretty tight parameters. "Beautiful" meant being tall and slim. It meant having long, slender legs. It meant straight, white teeth; a little nose; big eyes and smooth skin. "Beautiful" meant having boobs that weren't too big and weren't too small; and it definitely meant swishy hair. I could tick off a couple of things on that list, but most of them were too far beyond anything I could ever force my body to be.

But *why* was that my recipe for "beautiful"? The first part of this answer isn't especially ground-breaking: it's something most of us have understood for a long time now. My parameters for "beautiful" have described the majority of women I've always seen on the covers of magazines; in films; on my TV screen... we all understand that women who look a certain way are most likely to be hailed as beautiful and thrust into the public eye as an unattainable comparison for the rest of us. You probably already know and understand this. You probably also already know that those beautiful women have often had their images airbrushed before we see them; or have had a team of hairdressers and make-up artists, personal trainers and stylists... and that they don't wake up looking like the astonishing goddesses presented to us. So it's no great surprise that we spend so much of our lives believing we can't feel beautiful... because we'll never look in the mirror and see a reflection that fits within those narrow limitations that you just can't help believing in, despite your logical, rational brain shouting at you: *"But it's not real!"*

So, we see a particular woman of a particular shape and size and colour, and we see variations of the same woman again and again... with the same message again and again: *"This is what beautiful is!"* And those messages go so much deeper. This is the surface message, but actually what we take from it isn't just "this is what beautiful is"... it's "this is what *normal* is". When you look *nothing* like those women – which, let's face it, is most of us – when you're short, fat and bald; when your nose, bum, thighs or boobs are the wrong shape; when your cheeks are too pink or your hair is too frizzy; when your skin is wrinkled or liver-spotted; when your tummy hangs over your knickers… when you have *any* physical attributes that don't fit within those narrow parameters of *beautiful* you believe that they're *wrong*, and you believe that the way you look isn't normal. You believe you don't look like other women.

When my hair fell out, I'd never met another bald woman. Occasionally – *very* occasionally – I'd see one on TV, but by and large my screens continued to be filled with women sporting lustrous hair. And so my feelings of *unbeautifulness* were compounded by the fact I felt so alone. Every time I saw my naked head in the mirror it looked alien to me, and filled me with a sense of shame that I looked so very, very different from what was "normal". It all changed when I found a Facebook group run by the charity Alopecia UK. Suddenly, bald heads became my "norm". Every day I would scroll through the page, looking at photo after photo of women who looked like me. And each time I saw one, I had the same thought. "She looks so beautiful." Young and old, slim and round, every face took on a powerful beauty without hair. The more I saw those photos, the more I began to feel more normal. And the more I felt normal, the closer I got to feeling beautiful.

It's so hard to feel beautiful when you believe there are parts of your body that aren't normal. When there are parts of you that aren't how women are "supposed" to look. But you can change that. In the next Guided Reflection I'm going to ask you to seek out other women who look like you: but I need to offer a couple of warnings before you start. Firstly, when you search online for women who share the same features that make you feel *unbeautiful* there is every chance that the first results you find will be ones confirming that you're right to dislike that physical trait. If you search, for example, for "women with saggy breasts" you are likely to find results that offer you a solution... a solution to something that your search term never claimed to be a problem! Scroll past the results offering you surgery and exercise programmes, and hunt out the photos and articles that remind you that it's normal for your breasts to sag. And stay mindful of what's happening here... no wonder you've learned to believe it's wrong to have saggy breasts if these are the first messages you see when you seek reassurance that you're normal.

The second warning comes by way of photo filters. When sharing photos on social media it has become the norm for so many of us to add a filter. Not only to our own faces... to everything. This, of course, makes the task of finding pictures of women like you even trickier. So, as you search through images for the next Guided Reflection, be mindful that women who look too good to be true probably are. You might be in the habit of doing it yourself. Be honest: are you one of the people who adds a filter to photos of yourself, your cat and your skinny cappuccino? Maybe it's time to challenge yourself to let the world – and more importantly, to let other women – see you as you are. Because *they're* looking at *your* filtered photos feeling inadequate too.

Guided Reflection 21:

What parts of yourself do you feel stop you from achieving your True Goal of feeling beautiful? Write down as many as you want to: it's important you're really honest with yourself. When I've done this work with clients their answers have been wide ranging and included overhanging tummies; back fat; moles; crooked teeth; scars and thinning hair.

It can be painful to write this list, but it's important to address the negative beliefs you have about certain parts of your body. The next part of this Guided Reflection is very important and will help you to normalise the features you don't usually get to see represented.

Find other women who share those features and traits. Doing an online image search is a great place to start. Find as many photos as you can of other women who have moles, scars, or back fat. Print them out if you want to, and write down some descriptions of what you're seeing. Finally, think of an affirmation you can write down: choose reassuring words that will help you to remember that there are so many other women who look how you do. For example:

"It is normal to have a saggy tummy. So many women have a saggy tummy, and they are beautiful."

"So many women have a **saggy tummy,** and they are **beautiful**".

Do you see what I mean about having to scroll past all the offers to "fix" you? If you found that tough (and who would blame you), ask yourself an important question. How many industries depend on your belief that you need to be "fixed"? How much money can be made from making women believe there is only one way to look "right" and that the answer to achieving it is just one product, course, or procedure away? *It is in those industries' interests to stop you from seeing women who look like you.*

As soon as you realise your body is normal, you stop needing those industries. So, the last Guided Reflection is something you should do often. It's not an exercise that's about feeling beautiful, it's about feeling normal. Because how can you possibly go on to feel beautiful until you truly believe that you are absolutely fine the way you are?

Once you've opened your eyes to a thousand different ways that a woman can be normal, you can then begin to challenge yourself to widen your own parameters of what constitutes *beautiful*. You can begin to see the beauty in all kinds of bodies and faces, and you can start to understand that you don't have to change a single thing about your own body to be allowed to call it beautiful.

None of this is to say, of course, that you *can't* change how you look if you want to. Whether it's a daily transformation through the use of make up; whether you want to change your shape by losing weight; whether it's colouring your hair, or fake-tanning your skin; or wearing contact lenses instead of glasses, or braces on your teeth; whether it's having a boob job or a nose job; whether you choose to change your appearance with tattoos and piercings… it's your body, and your choice. The important question to ask is *why*. Are you altering your natural state to hide how you look? Is it from shame, embarrassment or self-loathing? Or does it come from a place of self-love? It is an act of kindness, and of respecting your body and your self-expression?

I have always enjoyed wearing make-up, for example,

but the reasons for it have changed. In my teenage years I used make-up to create a character: thick black eye make-up and bright red lipstick created a "mask" that I hid behind. I hoped that people would see the make-up instead of looking deeper and seeing the real me. Without make-up I felt vulnerable and open to judgement, so I used it to create a barrier to protect me. Now, twenty-five years later, I still wear make-up most days: but it's because I *want* people to look at me. I wear bright colours on my eyes – oranges, greens and pinks. I use make-up as an expression of my confidence and positivity. And the time I spend getting it right is an act of self-care. It's a little pocket of time each day spent pampering myself and reminding myself I am worth investing in.

It's important to remember that two different women can be doing exactly the same thing to their bodies but for different reasons and with different meanings. For example, two of my clients were both avid gym-goers. One was going because she was desperate for a flat tummy. She had convinced herself that she would never get a boyfriend until her stomach was tight and toned, and so she forced herself to join her local gym and work tirelessly at getting the tummy she thought she needed to have before she could be loved. The other client goes to the gym four times a week because she loves and respects her body. She sees her gym time as the ultimate in self-care and in prioritising her health and happiness above anything else. She wants to be able to be fit and healthy and run around with her kids; and whilst she prides herself on being there for the people she loves, she never lets that encroach on her gym time, which is sacrosanct.

Guided Reflection 22:

Write a list of all the things you do that change how you look in some way. Some might be small things, like wearing mascara every day, getting false nails or colouring your hair. Some might be bigger things such as losing weight or having cosmetic surgery. Maybe you regularly wear control underwear that disguises your natural shape, or perhaps you always add a filter to your photos before sharing them on social media. Write as many things as you can think of.

Then, for each one, rate the following statements from 1 to 10. The higher the number, the more you agree:

- I do this because I'm scared not to.
- I do this because it makes me feel good.
- I do this because I feel like I ought to.
- I do this because I love and respect myself.

Reflect on your answers. Can you identify which things you do for positive reasons, and which ones are done for negative reasons? If you're changing your appearance and it's driven by fear or obligation, it's time to think about whether you want to carry on doing that.

This is why you shouldn't compare the changes you make to your own appearance to those that other women work on. Some use make-up to hide like I used to, and some use it because they are positive and proud, like I do now. Some go to the gym through fear (like my first client) and some see it as the ultimate in self-care (like my second client). So much of what we do to ourselves is driven by what other women are doing: one client even told me she was considering a face lift simply because other women in her friendship group were having them! But the driving forces behind those physical changes are different for each of us. Back in the amazing Facebook group that introduced me to so many beautiful bald women: some wear wigs because they are terrified people will realise they have alopecia. And some wear wigs because they are embracing the fun of trying different hair styles and colours, and are enjoying the attention their new hair brings them.

So… *what is beautiful anyway*? You will have your own ideas, but it's time to challenge yourself. Try widening your parameters. Try finding women who look like you and finding the beauty in them. Try reminding yourself that your view of "beauty" has been influenced by those who profit from you believing you need to look different. Try telling yourself that you don't need to change anything about how you look unless it makes you feel good to do it.

What is beautiful? *You* are beautiful. *I* am beautiful. None of us fit into those tight, superficial parameters. But we are beautiful anyway.

CHAPTER 10

Beautiful in the End

How do you want to feel about the way you look when you're an old lady? It's probably not something you've ever thought about before. And it's not a question I'd ever considered until recently, when I visited my 87-year-old nanna. She asked me, as she always does, how my business is going and whether I had plenty of clients. I was happy to be able to tell her about the difference I've been making to the way so many women see themselves, and then I told her I'm writing a book. "What's it called?" she asked me. "*How to Feel Beautiful*!" I told her. And without missing a beat, Nanna replied, "I need to read that then!"

Later I mused over this conversation. I realised I'd assumed that I would have stopped caring about such trivial things as my appearance when I'm in my eighties. I went to my Facebook group *How to Feel Beautiful* and asked whether my members expected to care less about beauty when they reached old age. The answer was a resounding "no". One woman shared that her 82-year-old mum won't leave the house without lipstick. Another said that she cares just as much about her appearance now as she did twenty years ago, but the visible signs of ageing are making her feel worse. And another member explained that her mother had asked for her eyebrows to be tattooed for her ninetieth birthday present so that they could look less sparse. The most revealing comment was from Donna who told us about her nanna who, in her nineties, was hospitalised after falling off her bathroom scales. Donna said:

> "This naturally stunning, slim and statuesque woman, known for her beauty, was so conditioned by a number that she put herself literally in mortal danger to feed a widely shared obsession."

Donna's nanna's story is one that really struck a nerve with me. A lifetime of conditioning to meet certain physical criteria caused her to put herself in danger. Donna's nanna... my own nanna... made me realise. None of us will get to eighty years old and suddenly – magically – feel beautiful and confident. It's what you do between now and then that will determine whether that becomes your reality. It's time to ask yourself some tough questions about what kind of old lady you want to be, and to create a clear picture in your mind of the distant future you would love to become your reality.

Welcome to my distant future...

Lizi sat in her favourite armchair, surrounded by her family. Children and stepchildren, grandchildren and nieces... they all gathered around as Jacob lit the candles on his elderly mum's birthday cake. The eight and the zero crackled and sparkled on the pink icing as everyone began singing.

Lizi beamed at them all, smoothing down the silver blouse she'd bought for the occasion – never too old to show off a little cleavage! The deep wrinkles around her eyes were evidence of a lifetime of laughter, contrasted against the smoothness of her hairless head. She still made the time to draw on her eyebrows each morning: a little act of self-love that made her feel good. As the singing came to an end, Lizi's great-grandchildren ran to cuddle her, enjoying the warm familiarity of her soft, plump stomach and big arms as they squeezed her and kissed her creased, silken cheeks. The smallest child reached up to place a homemade crown on his great-grandmother's head and they all laughed at how silly and beautiful she looked.

Lizi thought of all the birthdays that had gone before. She thought about her tenth birthday party, wearing a dress made for her by her grandmother: a dress made for twirling in. She thought about her eighteenth birthday party: fancy dress so that she could hide behind a costume. She thought about the birthdays where she had longed for attention from boys; birthdays where the signs of ageing had begun to bother her; and birthdays where she'd cried because the clothes she'd bought hadn't looked right. She thought of her fortieth birthday – the last birthday at which she'd had hair – and thought about how unnecessary all the tears had been.

She had never lost the desire to look good, but knew now that she was (and always had been) beautiful. She looked across at Luke, sitting in the next armchair. His blue eyes twinkled at her. After forty-one years of marriage he still made her feel like the most beautiful girl in the world. She thought of all the years she'd spent trying to change and reflected on how much happier the second half of her life had been, once she was on her journey of loving herself exactly as she was. Lizi looked around at her eightieth birthday party and felt content and loved… and beautiful.

Guided Reflection 23:

Imagine yourself in the future. Imagine yourself as the old lady *you hope to be* one day. Write a description of yourself, as though you are looking at yourself from the outside.

Creative writing might be something you really enjoy, in which case – go for it! If it's something you find a little more difficult here are some prompt questions. Use them to help you create a full and vivid picture of yourself as the old lady you want to be.

- Where is she, and why?
- What is she doing?
- What is she wearing?
- What does she look like?
- What is she thinking?
- How is she feeling?

Really try to put yourself in the mind of that future version of you. You might be surprised at what you end up writing: I know I surprised myself when I did it.

And there she is. The version of you that you one day hope to be. She *can* be your reality... but it's up to you to decide. You won't suddenly reach eighty and stop giving a fuck about how you look. You need to put the work in *now*. Learn to love yourself in all your beautiful glory, right here and now, and old-lady-you will be so glad you did.

If you're wondering whether it's possible to reach old age and feel amazing in your own skin let me tell you about Eve, another member of my Facebook group. She commented in the group, telling us that she is eighty-three years old, weighs 220lbs... *"and I know I'm sexy"*. We had a conversation in the group as I asked her the secret to feeling beautiful and sexy in your eighties. Eve shared some incredible advice with us all. *"Be your own best friend,"* she told us. She recalled that a doctor once told her that women get up in the morning and point

"Be your own best friend"

out everything they don't like about themselves, but Eve does the opposite. And here she is… a sexy octogenarian who feels as beautiful as we would *all* love to feel.

Eve is your reminder that the story you wrote about old-lady-you is possible. You know exactly how you want to be when you are her age. Read back what you wrote about your distant (or not so distant) future on a regular basis. Keep that picture of your old-lady-self in your mind, and carry her with you in your heart. And any time this important work you're doing feels too difficult… summon her up in your mind's eye and tell her *"I'm doing this for you."*

CHAPTER 11

Mind Your Language

For fuck's sake, why are you just sitting there reading? Is that really the best use of your time? You've got so many other things you should be doing right now! The dishwasher needs loading, the washing needs folding, your email inbox needs your attention and you've got a pile of paperwork to deal with. Anyone else would have done all this stuff by now! Why are you so bloody lazy? You're never on top of your workload, and you've let so many friends down who want some of your time: they must all really hate you by now. Why can't you be more like other women? They seem to manage OK, so why can't you? Why can't you just do better?

Ouch. That was really uncomfortable to write, and I'm guessing it was unpleasant to read. Because, of course, I would never really talk to you like that – and hopefully you know that it wouldn't be OK for me or anyone else to do that. And yet. You *do* let someone talk to you like this, on a daily basis. That person is *you*.

You don't use those exact words, of course. Maybe you criticise yourself for not getting through your to-do list, or for failing to go to the gym, or for choosing takeaways over home-cooked dinners. Perhaps you give yourself a hard time for not being clever enough, brave enough or outspoken enough. Maybe you tell yourself you're not a good enough mum, wife, daughter, sister or friend? Or do you put yourself down for your physical appearance? Do you use words like gross, wrinkly, saggy or ugly when you talk about yourself?

The language we use when we talk *to* ourselves and *about* ourselves is powerful. The more you say it and the more you think it, the more you believe it. Let's try a little experiment so I can show you what I mean. In a moment, close your eyes and repeat to yourself a few times, either out loud or silently in your head: "*I'm a failure. I let everyone down. I'm a failure. I let everyone down.*" Do it six or seven times before you open your eyes again. Go.

How does your energy feel right now? I'm sorry for making you do something so uncomfortable, but it's important for you to understand the power you have to alter the way you feel. Let's try it again but this time let's lift your mood. This time repeat the words: "*I am beautiful. I'm unstoppable. I am beautiful. I'm unstoppable.*" Again, close your eyes and repeat it a number of times. Go.

Once again now, take a minute to assess how your energy feels. It's different, isn't it? Those positive words can make you feel more upbeat and happy, and more able to deal with the stresses and challenges of life; they can increase your self-belief and confidence and alter your entire mentality to become one where anything feels possible.

It really is this easy to give yourself a positive boost and change your mindset for the better… but it's also this easy to change it for the worse.

You may think I'm immune to this. I spent years working on my own confidence and self-esteem before becoming a coach and helping other women to do the same. But even now – during the very week that I wrote this chapter – I fell foul of the negative self-talk that can creep in without us even realising we're doing it. With a family wedding coming up I wanted to treat myself to a new dress – and having ordered a few options online that all needed to be returned for various reasons, I decided to head to my local shopping centre and enjoy a happy morning to myself, ambling around the shops and trying on dresses until I found the perfect wedding outfit. That was the plan, anyway. The reality was quite different.

After two hours I had only found a grand total of three dresses available in the size 20 that I needed. Three dresses for me to try on. And none of them suited me. I went from shop to shop, growing more and more disheartened: the final straw was an assistant in a popular clothing chain telling me their "Curve" range was only available online. I felt my face burning red, furious at the decision to prevent plus-size women trying on clothes before buying them. No matter how much confidence you've got… a shopping experience in which every store, every dress, every mannequin screams: *"Your body is WRONG!"* can be enough to give that confidence an almighty dent. And so, the negative thoughts began creeping in.

"It's your own fault for putting on all the weight you lost. If you weren't so undisciplined you wouldn't have got fat again. For fuck's sake, Lizi… you worked so hard to lose all that weight. How can you have let yourself down so badly? Everyone knew you'd put it back on again – they must all be laughing at you now. Look at all these beautiful dresses! But they're not for you. They're made for women with great bodies. And what on earth are you going to look like at the wedding? All the bride's skinny friends will be looking at you. They'll all look fashionable and sexy; and you'll look terrible. And you've got no-one to blame but yourself. If you're going to let yourself turn into a big fat pig, then this is what you get."

The more I allowed those thoughts in – the more space I gave them in my head – the more I believed them. And whilst I know with complete certainty that those things are not true, in that moment that was what I told myself and that was what I believed.

Of course, we all do this to some extent. We all allow negative thoughts to creep in and we all tell ourselves from time to time that we're not enough, in one capacity or another. We've all forgotten an appointment, or missed our exit on the motorway, or been late for an important deadline, and muttered to ourselves: *"You stupid idiot!"* Everyone does this: it's normal. But it's *not* normal to do it until it creates real, lasting damage to your confidence and self-esteem.

So… I'm not going to tell you to stop saying unkind

things to yourself, because as nice as that would be, it's probably unrealistic. What I *am* going to do is show you how to stop that negative self-talk in its tracks, before it has time to have a lasting impact. It all starts with training yourself to notice when you're doing it. It begins with listening to the words you're using when you mentally put yourself down.

Take my shopping trip, for example. After a few hours of feeling steadily worse about myself, I gave up on trying to find a dress and went home. I felt miserable and tearful. I was aware of a painful sadness, mingling with anger and frustration. I was angry at the situation… but also felt angry with myself. So, I sat quietly and asked: "What am I telling myself?" And I wrote it down.

"It's all my fault I can't find a dress to wear."

I read the sentence a few times. Was it true? Was it really my fault? I asked myself what the evidence was to say that it was my fault, and wrote down my answers.

"When I lost weight, I had much more choice available to me. I was able to buy clothes because I loved them, not just because I was grateful they fitted me. I've gained the weight back because I ate too much and stopped exercising. I stopped prioritising my health and wellbeing. If I hadn't done that, I'd have been able to find a dress today."

Clarifying my thoughts like this was helpful. Rather than a confused mixture of feelings I was able to understand exactly what was bothering me so much. I went on to ask myself for the evidence that my initial thought was wrong: the evidence that it *wasn't* all my fault that I couldn't find a dress.

"*The department store I was in should have catered better for a range of sizes. If the average UK dress size is a 16 then at a 20 I'm only two sizes above that: the equivalent of a size 12 going in the other direction. I saw dozens of dresses in a size 12. I deserve to be equally represented. My body deserves to wear nice things. It is my fault that I've gained weight, but that has nothing to do with finding a dress today – because whether I'm a size 12 or a size 20, I deserve to be valued and given the opportunity to find clothes I love. It is the store's fault that I couldn't get a dress. I deserved a much better experience today.*"

Lastly, I took my original thought: "*It's all my fault I can't find a dress to wear,*" and thought about how I could re-word it to make it more accurate, and reflective of my evidence. I decided on:

"*I have gained weight and the shop did not stock many dress options in my size. The problem today was with the store and the clothing choices, not with my body.*"

And with that important exercise, the way I felt about myself completely changed. I'd gone from self-hatred to self-love. I'd gone from being angry *with* myself to being angry *for* myself.

Guided Reflection 24:

Think of a time – preferably recently – when you were unkind to yourself. Write down the exact thought you were having. Some examples of negative thoughts my clients have had are:

- I'm fat and ugly
- No-one likes me
- I never do anything right

Or your example might be related to a specific event, like my own example above.

Once you've done that, reflect on your words for a few minutes. How does it feel to see them written down? Do you still believe them to be true?

Next ask yourself: *Where is the evidence that this is true?* Write down your answers.

Now ask yourself: *Where is the evidence that this is not true?* Write down your answers.

Finally, reflect on how you feel about your original statement and rewrite it to make it more accurate.

This, my lovely, is the single most important part of your journey to feeling beautiful. I *feel* beautiful because I *tell myself* I am beautiful. I've stopped making self-deprecating jokes about my weight. I've stopped using negative words to describe the way I look. And I've started deliberately choosing to describe myself in positive ways – both to myself and to others.

I tell my children that I am beautiful. I look in the mirror and consciously tell myself I look gorgeous. I notice all the bits of me that are lovely. And the bits I still struggle with sometimes… my tummy… my thighs… I *make* myself be nice about them. I notice the soft smooth skin on my tummy. I stroke the dimples on my thighs. I use words like strong and warm and adorable when I consciously think about them. *Feeling* beautiful starts with *thinking* beautiful and *speaking* beautiful.

But why is it so difficult to do? In my Facebook group *How to Feel Beautiful* I asked the members whether they would describe themselves as beautiful. I'm happy to say that some said yes, but there was an overwhelming feeling that it was wrong to do so. That it was conceited and immodest to say "I am beautiful". That it makes us bad people. And that if we do – tentatively – try saying it, it feels embarrassing. These were all feelings that I recognised in my younger self, but I couldn't quite pinpoint *why* it would feel so negative to say something so positive.

Until one incredible lady, Shira, made a comment in my group that completely explained it. She has given me permission to share her words here:

"No wonder so many of us have major self-esteem issues when we're raised to believe that self-esteem is itself a negative character trait, especially for girls and women. I realised a few years ago how deep this conditioning goes, and how we're taught to use it against people, when a friend of mine posted a selfie and captioned it with "I'm pretty". My conditioned mental response was "Yes, you are, but is there any need to say that?" and I was like "Wow, brain, really? There's *every* need for her to say that."

What a revelation. Girls are taught that they should be humble and modest. We think that it's an insult to say, "She's got such a high opinion of herself!" But I'm ready to say, "Fuck humility and fuck modesty. I'm fucking beautiful!"

So… are you ready to cast off all those old beliefs? Are you ready to start being mindful of the language you use about yourself, and to start replacing negative self-descriptions with positive ones? Because I have to tell you, my lovely… you're not going to feel beautiful until you do.

Over the years, I have had so many beautiful women sit at my coaching table with me in tears. Women who are truly, physically, stunning… but who just can't see it. Sitting next to short, fat, bald *me*, in all my beautiful glory. And time and time again that same picture provides incontrovertible proof of what I've said before, and will say again:

"Feeling beautiful has nothing to do with how you look, and everything to do with how you look at yourself." – Lizi Jackson-Barrett

"Feeling beautiful has nothing
to do with how you look,

and everything to do with

how you look at yourself."

And yes, I did just quote myself there: because this is one of the most important things I've ever said! Feel free to quote me too… your friends need to hear this, again and again.

The most important thing is how you look at yourself. And you have complete power over how you *look* at yourself by changing how you *speak* to yourself. *This* is the secret you've been waiting to learn. I couldn't tell you earlier because you wouldn't have understood. You had to do the work first – on understanding your dreams and goals and creating new habits; on building your circles of support and choosing to prioritise your happiness. And now, my lovely, you're ready. Now you know the truth, that it's all been about one thing: showing yourself the unconditional love that you deserve.

Now you know how to feel beautiful.

CHAPTER 12

The Right Fairytale

Once upon a time there was a magical princess. She was You.

The princess was born with endless, infinite potential. Everyone loved and adored her completely and unconditionally. She did not spend time questioning her self-worth. No-one commented that she would be such a beautiful baby if she could just lose a little weight or grow her hair a bit longer, or if her nose was straighter or her eyelashes longer. Her deep power and innate beauty were just known. She knew it instinctively with a true and honest knowing, because like all princesses she was born with a special magic that allowed her to see herself the way others saw her and granted her the ability to see a mighty and mysterious beauty that lay within her very soul.

But one day – way too soon, before the magical princess was even fully grown – a wicked witch appeared. The witch cast a spell, which planted a very dangerous thought in the princess's mind. The thought was: "I am not beautiful". It was a dark and potent spell, which made the princess forget her own magic and clouded her thoughts every day. In an instant the princess had lost her quiet trust in her beauty and now thought only of what she was lacking. The princess didn't realise she had been bewitched and unquestioningly believed the thought lodged in her mind by the wicked witch. She didn't like feeling that she was not beautiful. It made her very sad.

As the magical princess grew older, she would gaze longingly out of the window of the tallest tower in her castle. She watched all the other princesses across the land and saw that they were beautiful. Each of them had their own unique beauty that the princess so admired. So, she tried to change herself to be more like them, so that she might rid herself of those dark, sad thoughts implanted deeply in her mind by the wicked witch. She attended grand balls just as the other princesses did, wearing long silk gowns and sparkling tiaras... and hoped no-one would look beneath the surface to discover how far from beautiful she really was.

What the princess didn't know was that the wicked witch had cast the same spell over all the other princesses in the land. They looked at each other and saw that every other princess was so very beautiful, but were each blind to their own beauty. They looked at the magical princess and saw so much beauty. So, all the princesses put on their most glamorous gowns and tiaras, smiled their most princessy smiles, and prayed no-one would see what they knew to be true: that they alone were not beautiful.

For many years the magical princess lived this life. Occasionally she would recall tiny glimpses of the magic she had forgotten, and the witch's spell would momentarily lift. In those moments the princess would see with absolute clarity that she had been cursed and that the sad, dark feelings about her beauty were not true. But no-one had taught the princess how to use her own magic and so she couldn't sustain it, and then the witch's evil enchantment would settle and take hold once more.

One day – a day not so very different from the thousands that had gone before it – a fairy godmother appeared. She explained to the magical princess that she had been cursed many, many years ago. The princess was overjoyed at the thought that the fairy godmother had come to release her from the grip of the evil spell; but was also frightened. The thought that she was not beautiful was all she could remember thinking, so how could she live a life without it?

Then the fairy godmother continued, and the princess understood that it would not be so easy for her to be rid of the evil curse. The fairy godmother explained that the wicked witch had grown stronger over the years and had invented new ways for princesses to instantly compare themselves with each other to fortify the beliefs implanted by her spell. The witch had ensured that merely looking at each other intensified the princesses' beliefs that they alone were not beautiful. The wicked witch was very clever, the godmother said, because the spell had become so enmeshed in the mind of the magical princess that it was impossible to disentangle it, and that even a fairy as powerful as the godmother was unable to remove it completely. However, the godmother whispered lovingly to the magical princess, there was one important secret that even the wicked witch did not understand.

Simply knowing that the spell was there was enough to diminish its power.

So, the magical princess became very still; and listened intently to the whispering of her heart. And true enough, she heard it. An almost imperceptible murmur, like a mellow summer wind: her heart told her that the dark, sad thoughts were not true and never had been. And the magical princess found herself thinking an unfamiliar thought: "What if I am beautiful? What if I have been beautiful all along?"

"I cannot extinguish the spell," said the fairy godmother, "but I can teach you how to make it so small that most of the time you barely notice it. It won't be easy and sometimes you will doubt that it is even possible; but I will stay by your side and help you, especially on the days when the spell's lies feel more like truth.

"What the wicked witch does not know," the fairy godmother continued, "is that every princess is born with her own special and powerful magic; more potent than the witch's evil curse. It is the same magic that you have fleetingly seen in moments so brief they scarcely felt real. They are real, my darling. Those moments of magic can become your reality if you trust me." The fairy godmother promised the magical princess that she would help her to use her own magic to fight the wicked witch's spell, and the princess felt an electrifying thrill at the thought that she might be able to finally let go of the belief that she was not beautiful enough.

And so together the magical princess and her fairy godmother began to understand the princess's own magic. It was a magic that hid in unexpected places and the princess had to learn how to look for it and recognise it before she could use it. At first, she would cry in frustration as she would lose her grasp on the tantalising magic that kept the witch's curse at bay. But the more she understood it, the more she used it. The thought that she was not beautiful never fully disappeared because, as the fairy godmother had explained, it was too tangled in the princess's mind to permanently leave her. But her special and powerful magic eventually made the evil spell so insignificant that she was finally able to enjoy the limitless potential that had always been part of who she was. At last, the magical princess was able to move forward on her life's path, complete with the understanding that she had always been beautiful but had simply forgotten how to see it.

Many, many years later, the magical princess sat in her peaceful garden, enjoying the warmth of the sun on her closed eyelids and her delicately wrinkled face. The silver-white threads of her fine hair glinted in the sunlight. "Grandmother?" came a

little voice. The princess opened her eyes and smiled at the small girl standing before her, offering a freshly-picked buttercup. "What were you dreaming about, Grandmother?" The magical princess scooped the child onto her lap and embraced her tightly with twisted, speckled hands. "I dreamed about being your age again, my darling. I dreamed that I could tell my small self everything I know now. I dreamed I told her a very special and important secret that helped her to truly love her powerful, glorious self; never questioning her own magic and beauty."

"The secret, Grandmother? Oh, tell me! I love secrets!" The magical princess smiled again. "You don't need me to tell you my darling. You already know."

~~The End~~
The Beginning

Acknowledgements

There's only one place to start here… and that's with my incredible children, Jacob and Layla, and my gorgeous husband Luke: the most beautiful humans I know. Without the unconditional support, love and encouragement you give me I'd never have found the strength and courage to love myself as much as you all do. Thank you for constantly seeing the beauty in me and showing me what I couldn't always see in myself.

Thank you also to my beautiful friends – more like sisters – who are numerous and wonderful. I am so very grateful to have so many of you cheering me on when I'm winning and picking me up when I fall. I can't name you all (and I know how deeply lucky I am to have too many true friends to list) but I am especially thankful to have Vicky, Kate, Rachel, Debbie, Ceit, Laura and Viv in my life. You all mean more to me than you know.

I am so grateful to everyone who helped make this book a reality, and especially my beautiful and inspirational book mentor, Cassandra Farren from Welford Publishing. Thank you, Cassie, for being my guide as I put my experience into words. Thank you for helping me to trust myself; for reassuring and encouraging me; and for the gentle ass-kicking when I needed it! Thank you also to the wonderful Jen Parker from Fuzzy Flamingo for your vision and creativity. Thank you for turning my manuscript into an actual book and for making it look so incredible. And thank you to Gabrielle Vickery for your beautiful illustrations, and for bringing moments of my book to life in such a special and unique way.

Thank you also to Alopecia (something I never imagined myself saying). When you came into my life I was so scared of you, and thought you'd appeared to destroy me. I was wrong. You arrived to teach me so many important things about my own strength, resilience and beauty. You gave me the chance to show my children there is more than one way to be beautiful, and the opportunity to help countless women with their own body confidence struggles. And thank you to the charity Alopecia UK – a group that is so important to those feeling alone in their journey, and a community that was there for me when I needed them most.

And finally, thank you to all the powerful, vulnerable, strong, fearful, beautiful women who allow me to support them on their own journeys to loving themselves fully. Thank you for opening your hearts to me and trusting me to help you to see how beautiful you truly are. You all inspire me more than you can know.

Contact Me

I would love to hear from you!

You might like to tell me about the effect this book has had on you (I'm excited to know!); or perhaps it's left you with questions that you'd like to ask. Maybe you want to find out about having coaching with me, either on a one-to-one basis or as part of one of my online groups. Or do you want to enquire about booking me as a speaker for your event or organisation? Whatever it is, I'm looking forward to hearing from you.

You can reach me at lizi@lizijacksonbarrett.com

Want to find out more about me and what I do?

My website is:
  www.lizijacksonbarrett.com

Or follow me at:
  www.facebook.com/lizijacksonbarrett
  www.instagram.com/lizijacksonbarrett

Join the conversation:

You'll have noticed that I've mentioned my free Facebook group a number of times over the course of the book, and I would love to invite you to join us. Come and take part in important, uplifting and supportive discussions about what it means to be and feel beautiful:

www.facebook.com/groups/HowToFeelBeautiful

About Lizi

Lizi lives in Essex, England, with her husband Luke, ten-year-old twins Jacob and Layla, and two cats Upsy Daisy and Minerva. Sometimes her teenage step-kids Luke Jr and Alyssa join them. Lizi loves it when they're all together, and loves it when she's on her own too.

Lizi was a secondary school teacher for eight years but discovered that her favourite part of the job happened outside of lessons, when students came to her to talk through their worries. So she retrained as a coach, gaining a Postgraduate Diploma in Coaching from the University of East London. She's now a successful coach transforming the way women see themselves, as well as a motivational speaker and freelance educator.

Lizi is on a mission to reach every woman who feels that "beautiful" is an unattainable dream, and who has spent their life constantly trying to change how they look to achieve the holy grail that is "beauty". Lizi's aim is to inspire and empower each of those women to embrace a different narrative about their body, and to recognise that they've been beautiful all along. Lizi really loves seeing the difference it makes to other women when she shares her own story of learning to love herself.

Lizi also loves Harry Potter, buying presents, singing, and being right. She hates mushrooms, ironing, waiting, and getting sneezed on. Lizi is proud that she's got a genius-level IQ, and that she knows every word of the musical *Wicked*. She's not so proud that she once went on a TV game show and got 41 + 5 wrong.

Printed in Great Britain
by Amazon